"This exciting book of sermons by women clergy is a powerful affirmation of the fact that the ordination of women has already brought to the Episcopal Church a fresh and vital understanding of the full message of the Gospel."

Cynthia Wedel
First woman president, World Council of Churches

"As a literary scholar, I am delighted to hear the voices of southern women speak of old concerns in a new form. As a person, I am deeply grateful that their words have changed my thinking about what it means to preach and be 'preached at.'"

Anne Goodwyn Jones
Associate Professor of English, University of Florida, Author of
Tomorrow is Another Day: The Woman Writer in the South, 1859-1936.

"In this marvelous volume we are in the presence of women of incredible power, enormous tenderness, boundless commitment, and endless promise. This book is called *Women of the Word*, and, by God, their words are good."

Sidney B. Simon
Professor, University of Massachusetts, Author of *Values Clarification*,
Meeting Yourself Halfway, and *Helping Your Child Learn Right From Wrong.*

WOMEN OF THE WORD

Contemporary Sermons by Women Clergy

The Rev. Janice M. Bracken
The Rev. Eloise Hally
The Rev. E. Claiborne Jones
The Rev. Camille S. Littleton
Lori M. Lowe
The Rev. Doris Graf Smith
The Rev. Barbara Brown Taylor

Edited by
The Rev. Charles D. Hackett

SUSAN HUNTER *Publishing*

Atlanta, Georgia

Publisher:
Susan Hunter

Editor:
The Rev. Charles D. Hackett
Candler School of Theology
Emory University

Vitae:
Amanda Clark Gable
Institute of Liberal Arts
Emory University

Copy editing:
Phyllis Mueller Cahoon
Ellen Caldwell
Bonnie Pike

Photography:
Lynda Greer

Design:
Susan Hunter

Typesetting:
Safriet & Chance

Published by
Susan Hunter Publishing
Atlanta, GA

Manufactured in the United States
of America

5 4 3 2

Library of Congress Cataloging
in Publication Data

Bracken, Janice M.; Hally, Eloise; Jones,
E. Claiborne; Littleton, Camille S.; Lowe,
Lori M.; Smith, Doris Graf; Taylor, Barbara
Brown.

Women of the word.

Includes index.
1. Episcopal Church – Sermons. 2. Anglican
Communion – Sermons. 3. Church year sermons.
4. Sermons, American.   I. Bracken, Janice M.,
1957-.   II. Hackett, Charles D.
BX5937.A1W66   1985   252'.03   84-52656
ISBN 0-932419-00-3

CONTENTS

GREETING

The scriptures are very clear that gifts are given to be shared. Whether it is the gift of life, of fortune, or of the Spirit, they are not to be hoarded or managed in a selfish way. So it is with the gift of proclamation.

As a priest accepts the responsiblity for a new ministry, the prayer said before the priest is greeted by the bishop and the congregation includes the words "in preaching, give me readiness of thought and expression." Preaching bears fruit only as the Word is proclaimed and as the Word is received.

In the pages that follow, the several preachers are sharing with us the inspiration and power of the Word spoken and the Word made flesh. While the additional gift of their personal presence is not available to the reader, the impact of their "readiness of thought and expression" is.

As Bishop, I am grateful to the authors that they have given us this opportunity to profit from their thoughts and expressions. By means of the printed word their gift and ours can be shared with the wider community.

Charles J. Child, Jr.
Bishop of Atlanta

PREFACE

Continuity resists change. Discontinuity welcomes it. With regard to the ordination of women, those Churches of self-conscious attachment to Catholic continuity are generally on the side of resistance. By contrast, Churches of the Reformed tradition generally have embraced it.

The Anglican 'via media' suffers the discomfort of struggling to embody ecclesiastically the paradox of continuity and discontinuity at the heart of the Gospel. On the one hand, we have no Gospel to heed without faithful continuity that preserves its call to repentance into the present and future. On the other hand, we have not heeded the very Gospel preserved to us without a readiness for personal and ecclesiastical discontinuity which repentance calls for.

Given the contemporary resurgence of Catholic self-consciousness in the liturgy and life of the Episcopal Church (the Anglican tradition in the U.S.A.), the wonder is that in 1976 we agreed to move beyond a tradition cherished in Catholic continuity for all the centuries of Christian presence in history. Henceforward we would ordain women to the priesthood and episcopate.

But the action was not inclusive as legislation. It simply made it legal to ordain women for those bishops of the Episcopal Church who wished to do so. Roughly two-thirds of our bishops said they would then. Nearly ten years later, the number of bishops who ordain women has grown. Still, there is not mandate in this Church that compels a bishop to ordain anyone — man or woman.

Nor is the action inclusive on the world scale among Anglicans. Hardly. Most of the nearly thirty autonomous national bodies in the Anglican Communion world-wide have declined to ordain women. The largest of us, the Church of England, has begun to stir in earnest, but the time for a decision on the matter remains some years away.

All of this is to ratify the decidedly Catholic reality of Anglican self-consciousness. And it grows. In 1789, the Anglicans who survived the American

Revolution incorporated as "The Protestant Episcopal Church in the United States of America." The term "Protestant" has not been dropped entirely, but our General Convention as of 1976 has recognized "The Episcopal Church" as an alternate and equally acceptable name designating the Church.

Again it remains a wonder to us who favored it then, and favor it still, that the Episcopal Church, increasingly devoted to historic continuity, should come down on the side of painful discontinuity in the ordination question.

It was indeed painful and costly — but not divisive at the top, where the ordaining power resides. Not one active bishop bolted the Church. The reason for this sturdy unity is implicit in Anglican understanding of paradox. We know, most of us, that the opposite of a great truth is not falsehood but another great truth. Continuity and discontinuity stand as equivalent though contending values. We know, most of us, that partisans need the other party in order to be whole as men and women in Christ. Though we are tempted to resolve conflict by demolishing the other side, or by detaching from it, the love of Christ constrains us — and affection for one another deepens.

Speaking personally, my own affection for brother bishops on the other side of the aisle has been enlarged greatly. And my affection for those whom I ordain to priesthood took on new proportions when I could include women. The several women whose sermons form the substance of this book have been my teachers and my friends. They have widened my appreciation of human competence, deepened my joy in being a bishop, and illumined my self-understanding as embracing both male and female attributes. Most of all, they have been the chief instruments in the enlargement of my understanding of God. It comes to me so clearly now that, of course, God is male and female.

As yet, we do not know quite how to say this in devotional and theological discourse. But no matter. It is the character of the paradox of continuity and discontinuity to enliven the Church. It forces us into untried tomorrows where we learn new things — in obedience to Christ whose promise is to make all things new.

Bennett J. Sims
Bishop of Atlanta, Retired
Institute for Servant Leadership
Candler School of Theology
Emory University

INTRODUCTION

In the Episcopal Diocese of Atlanta women number fewer than five percent of the clergy. In the nine years since women were first ordained, it has become evident that these women are exceptional preachers. This book is an effort to make samples of their preaching available to a wider audience.

At the same time, it is an effort to give the reader a glimpse of the minds and methods of seven extraordinary servants of God's Word.

The phenomenon of their ability, of course, raises questions of how and why. Do these women preach so well because of a common educational experience or process of vocational selection? Or is it because of something about the female experience which gives them a special sensitivity in the ministry of the pulpit? There is no single answer to these questions but some intriguing observations about these women give us a better sense of what is basic and unique about their work.

CANDLER CONNECTION

To begin with, all seven preachers share an association with Emory University. Six are graduates of the Candler School of Theology and the seventh, Barbara Taylor, received her bachelor's degree from Emory College and returned to Candler to serve on staff after taking her M. Div. from Yale. Certainly the Emory curriculum, with its attention to biblical exegesis and interpretation and its emphasis on self-knowledge as a crucial part of formation for ministry, has something to do with the sermons in this book. On the other hand, association with Emory is not the whole answer, because these women excelled as preachers in seminary. Indeed, two were winners of Candler's annual Smith Award: the senior preaching prize.

EXPERIMENT IN MINISTRY

Perhaps the answer is more basic and has to do with the way in which these people were selected for the ministry. In the Diocese of Atlanta, everyone who wishes to be ordained enters a selection process, the Experiment in Ministry, which takes more than a year. In this program, aspirants to the ministry are placed in intense situations of ministry such as hospitals, city housing projects, and gay bars, as well as parishes. As they rotate through these pressure cookers of human interaction, they meet weekly with their peers and two supervisors to reflect upon their understandings . . . of the people they meet, of each other, of themselves and of God . . . in these situations. Periodically, the group writes and shares evaluations; they evaluate themselves and one another.

In the course of this experience, propensities and gifts for ministry are sorted out. Together the supervisors, the group and the individuals decide who is suited for the ordained ministry. It is an anxious, sometimes painful experience. The people who enter the ministry from this program tend to value their self-hood as an instrument of ministry. They are, as a rule, able to use their own life-experiences to understand and deal with others. They tend to do theology and to go about ministry by beginning with a given human situation. They are usually far more empathic than judgmental. Generally, they know a good deal about their own foibles and failings and, at their best, understand themselves according to Luther's dictum that though we remain sinners, yet we are justified by God.

Again, however, the selection process these seven women shared is not the whole answer to their homiletic ability. Certainly, it has contributed to their humanness and, perhaps, to the gentle irony which appears in their work, but the men who are products of this same selection process do not seem to enjoy the same reputation as preachers.

THE FEMALE EXPERIENCE

Perhaps, then, the critical element is the female experience. On one level, it is easy to see how this might be so. Each of these women is a pioneer. Two invested themselves in the process of training for the ministry even before General Convention had decided that the Episcopal Church would ordain women. Each has entered her vocation knowing it is a life-long, uphill battle for acceptance in a culture which has traditionally denied ordination to women and in which prejudice and fear will often continue to block the recognition of her gifts. Like members of minorities everywhere in our society, women clergy feel that they must work harder and accomplish more than their male counterparts to have a chance at equal recognition. These seven women, members of a minority in the Church, are no exception. Like most women in seminary, their grades were far above average. But even if we grant that they are adventurers by nature, and that they have worked harder than their male peers to acquire theological skills, that is still no assurance of preaching ability. A "cum laude" on a diploma has never guaranteed good sermons.

When we talk about the female experience are we talking about something more subtle, pervasive, and profound than being a minority in today's culture? When we raise this question, we are raising a series of issues so broad that even the growing discipline of "women's studies" cannot contain them. If we are going to look further for the shape and sources of the uniqueness and excellence of these sermons, we will have to turn to the sermons themselves. In the words of these seven women we look for the explicit and implicit theology that might tell us something of the female experience and, in turn, illuminate the whole human experience.

THEOLOGICAL METHODOLOGY AND THEMES

I introduce the word "theology" here intentionally. Each of these preachers brings to her task an implicit theology. This theology forms the way she looks at things from moment to moment. This theology is the reading lens she brings to every biblical text, the hearing aid she wears in every conversation, and the wide-angle glasses through which she attempts to see and make sense out of the chaotic manifold of human experience. In this way these seven clergy are like all the rest of us, for whether we reflect on it or not, we all interpret experience by means of a theology of some sort. Rudolf Bultmann said that exegesis without presuppositions was not possible. The same is true for all of life. We cannot interpret life's experiences without presuppositions, without a "grid" through which we can relate one experience to another and all of them to a sense of ourselves.

Because of this, every sermon is a kind of confession of faith, because every sermon exposes the sense of reality, the theology of the preacher. The act of preaching, then, is a considerable risk because one holds up for public scrutiny the very core of one's own being. In every sermon, the preacher says, "This is how it holds together for me." Each of these seven preachers begins with a presupposition that the gospel of Jesus Christ provides our best possibility for making sense out of things. And yet no theology is completely adequate; no sermon is complete or final. Rather, every sermon is an invitation as well as a confession. It is an invitation to dialogue. On one hand, it invites a dialogue between the hearer and his or her way of understanding things. It invites theological dialogue as Jesus invited dialogue when he told stories or undertook actions which confessed his way of understanding reality but did not mesh with the way his contemporaries saw things. It may even invite the kind of ultimate dialogue that Jesus undertook when he made his final confession of faith by submitting to the cross. To hear or read a sermon is to enter into a dialogue with the preacher and hopefully through that conversation enter into a second, deeper dialogue with the one whose way of understanding things is always radically different from ours.

If we are to read these sermons with the hope of deeper theological dialogue, then some theological orientation would be in order.

Despite their common connections, each of these seven preachers has her own distinctive way of coming at things. Each has her favorite themes which are clues to her theology. Eloise Hally begins with a passage of scripture and asks what such a thing could possibly mean for us. Both Claiborne Jones and Janice Bracken have an ability to "go with" biblical stories, trusting that these narratives will illuminate the narratives of our own lives. Lori Lowe shares this enthusiasm for story, but seems always to be hinting that God is working in and through the human story. If the Incarnation is thus implicit in her theology, it is explicit in Barbara Taylor. Doris Graf Smith ingeniously takes traditional themes and images and virtually plays with them until, by surprise, we find ourselves in the Gospel stories. Like others, Camille Littleton is willing to disclose her own anxiety that the world is disordered and baffling but does so to witness that there is divine unity and order at the center of things.

These are preliminary observations about method and theological themes. At this level, each is quite different from the others. What can be said that these preachers have in common when their work is given a second, closer, more comparative reading?

One observation is disarmingly simple but potentially profound. Every one of these sermons is in the indicative mood; not one of these sermons tells us what to do. The mood of the verbs is descriptive, not imperative. Such consistency seems particularly odd when one considers that conventional wisdom has it that sermons tell us what God wants us to do and often just how to do it.

THE IMPERATIVE TRADITION

The ancient kerygma of the Church very early on came to have an indicative and an imperative part. Listeners were told that: (1) Jesus who was crucified, risen, and soon to return was Messiah and therefore (2) they should repent and be baptised in his name.[1]

Paul's Epistles typically carry a paraenetic section, in which certain moral imperatives are given, based on the "particular" version of the "good news," which is tailored to the specific pastoral situation of the church to which Paul is writing. The preaching of the patristic age, couched in the rhetorical style of the time, moves back and forth between persuasion and exhortation. The accepted method for interpreting scripture in scholastic theology was a four-fold allegorical method, and the most important of the four "meanings" of scripture for preaching was the third, or "moral," level.[2]

Martin Luther, intoxicated as he was with the Gospel of God's having justified us while we were sinners utterly apart from our behavior, nevertheless, preached sermon after sermon redolent with exhortation based on how his hearers should respond to their having been so justified. Eighteenth-century preaching discovered the rational, deductive form of argument indigenous to the court of law and applied it in a clearly imperative manner. In the aridity of orthodox state-churches the exhortations had to do with obeying the moral law. In the pietistic alternative movements, the exhortations were to a certain discipline or a certain attitude. The great revival movements of the late 18th and 19th centuries exhorted to repentance following conviction and made the hallmark of such repentance a conversion which was known preeminently by a private, subjective experience of feeling. Thus, finally, hearers of sermons were exhorted to certain feeling-states.

The 20th century has reacted to this state of affairs pluralistically. Much theology and preaching has continued to exhort us to feel or behave in a certain way quite unabashedly. Other theologies have sensed something amiss in the imperative mode and have sought an alternative. One need only think of Paul Tillich's moving "un-exhortation" at the end of the sermon "You Are Accepted"[3] — we should now do nothing except know that we are accepted — in order to sense how difficult it is to preach without exhorting to *something*.

---

1. C.H. Dodd, *The Apostolic Preaching and its Developments* (London: Hodder & Stoughton, 1950).
2. Scripture was understood to have four allegorical meanings: literal, allegorical (or dogmatic), moral and anagogical (or mystical/eschatological).
3. Paul Tillich, *The Shaking of the Foundations* (New York: Charles Scribner's Sons, 1948), pp. 153-164.

Ours is a time when we have all become deeply suspicious of the imperative. Even if the anti-authoritarian atmosphere of the last decades seems to have dissipated, ours is a time in which authority is taken either desperately and naively or dismissed cynically. Since the imperative mood is the stock-in-trade of authority, ours is a time when the status of the exhortation is very much in question. It would seem that we must either accept and obey the imperatives of our authorities blindly and without question, or we must somehow find ourselves cut adrift without any sense of authority at all. In short, it seems that we are perilously like our forebears of the first half of the century, prey to ideologies and the obedience which follows from them. Every ideology, whether it is communism, fascism, capitalism, fundamentalism, or nationalism, has its attendant list of imperatives. The disconcerting result is that to preach in the imperative mood places Christian theology in the marketplace of ideologies, competing to sell itself on the same basis as nationalism. The fact that some segments of the religious community have done very well financially and numerically by entering this marketplace with a vengeance exacerbates the difficulty. To align the Church with any ideology (no matter how promising and right its imperatives may seem at any given moment), is inevitably to be found in the sin of idolatry.

For this reason, the indicative mood of these seven preachers has special significance. All are heirs of two different strains of the Christian tradition which may prove helpful to us at this point in history.

REVELATION IN THE INDICATIVE

Over the past few years, theologians have been rediscovering the indicative mood in narrative discourse. It has become commonplace to distinguish the form of the "story" as being a special kind of revelation. It has been argued that the story was typical of Jewish theology and that it has particular importance for us because it is inherently a "theology of history." Since Jesus was a Jew whose message was undoubtedly concerned with the form of history God was going to create, it is suggested that a narrative, historically oriented theology is inherently more valid than more revelational or prescriptive theologies.

The actual appeal of narrative theology, however, probably does not reside in its inherent superiority. Rather it attaches to the peculiarity of our time. In a moment in history when so many of us feel there is no one and nothing out there we can trust, and that the best we can do is somehow rely on our own life-experience, narrative theology can become very, very attractive. It is attractive because a listener can identify with a well-wrought story. Human existence is apparently so constructed that across time and across cultural gaps we can find our own experiences caught and reflected in the stories of others. In an age when we are cynical about whether we can communicate with anyone else, agnostic about whether we can believe anyone else, and consequently unsure even of how to get a veridical fix on our own experience, the discovery that there are others like us (in pulpits and in history), comes with almost salvific force. To find a preacher who can interpret Bible stories and articulate her or his own story in such a way that in them I find *my* story is surely to have found an authority in whom I might trust. Even better, the narrative form in and of itself does not provide for exhortation. A story just *is*. One may draw an interpretive implication from a story and add on a deduced imperative but, in and of itself, the narrative form stands in the indicative. The hearer is left to draw his or her own conclusions as to what the story "means."

In an entirely unexpected way, perhaps we are given a clue about why each of these women seems to tell stories so well. Perhaps here we catch a glimpse of one aspect of the "female experience." Throughout history, the story has belonged to the disenfranchised and officially powerless. The story of Scheherazade staving off her execution by spinning fascinating stories is a paradigm. The memories and hopes of conquered peoples without access to official means of communication are kept alive by sagas, ritual remembrances, and stories.

Throughout the history of the Church, women have been excluded from positions of power and authority. This was true in official Judaism of Jesus' time and it was true of the early Church. There were no women among the "Twelve." Women do not appear in the capacity of evangelist, baptizer, or layer-on of hands. Yet, women are ever a prominent part of the *narrative*. According to Luke, when Paul left Corinth for Syria he took with him "Priscilla and Aquila" (Acts 18:18). Women are mentioned frequently in the epistles, making it clear that they were crucial to the life and witness of the primitive Church.

Perhaps even more intriguing is the role women play in the Gospel narratives. Whether it is the woman with the ointment in Mark 14:3-9 or the place of Elizabeth, Mary, and the prophetess Anna in Luke's theology of salvation, women are accorded a place which is both revelational and salvific in the story of salvation itself. Nowhere is this more striking than in the empty tomb narrative in which in both the synoptic and Johannine traditions, Jesus' resurrection is discovered first by the two Marys — Mary, the mother of Jesus, and Mary Magdalene.

Evidence could be multiplied and certainly debated, but the provocative idea remains; women have been excluded from access to traditional ecclesiastical authority but they have been a crucial part of the *story* from the beginning. Their authority, like the authority of the story-form itself, has had to come from an intuitive ability to empathize and to speak the indicative word about the human situation in such a way that those who heard recognized their own being and their own dreams.

THE ANGLICAN PERSPECTIVE

The seven women represented by these sermons have a narrative skill and theological perspective in common. That perspective has much to do with their being Anglican.

Anglican theology is an elusive animal. Its history is entirely entwined with the history of England. It boasts no great theologians such as Luther or Calvin. Its most illustrious theological work was and is a prayer book produced by a theologian who often seemed hardly persuaded of anything except that a graceful use of the English language should be used for worship throughout the British Isles, even where English was not spoken, as in Wales. And yet there *is* an Anglican theology if we understand theology in the sense mentioned above, as a grid through which we make sense of reality.

Richard Hooker wrote theology in the 16th century. He wrote against the Puritans who wished to make England into a kind of enormous Geneva in which every phase of life would be governed by theological norms drawn from systematic interpretation of scripture. In reply, Hooker invoked a theology reminiscent of Thomas Aquinas. It was a natural theology and a derivative of medieval Catholic thinking. It took as its baseline the assumption that God's creation was good and though creation had been warped by sin, God was to be found at work in and through that creation, sustaining, redeeming, and re-creating.

Such a theology is inherently Incarnational in that it assumes God is somehow about the business of sustaining, redeeming, and re-creating in and through human activity and experience. Moreover, and very importantly, such a natural theology assumes that communication and understanding are possible. It is a theology which deeply mistrusts those who prescribe what must be done at all costs. It is chary of those who claim to have *the* truth. It wants, above all, to find the loci of God's activity in the world and move toward that activity to worship and cooperate. It always remembers that sin distorts our human perceptions and perverts our best intentions so that every human activity is ambiguous and relative. Human beings are asked, then, to take seriously and use every faculty available. Because the creation is essentially good, and because our part in the creation has been affirmed by the Incarnation, we are free to act as best as we can at any moment. Nevertheless, we must never think for a moment that what we understand or do is exactly true or unambiguously right. Instead, the ultimate end of things, the re-creation of all things, must be left to God who created all and is bringing all things to perfection.

This is a theology of moderation in which humanity takes its place in God's creation. As human beings, we are called upon to learn and act and live in creation, taking what we are and what we do seriously, but never as ultimate. In a sense, we are called on to be moderate in both our estimation and our judgment of ourselves and each other. Certainly such a theology can lead to complacency. The history of Anglicanism is full of sinful complacency. Yet for all of that, such a theology may be right for our time.

This theology informs the sermons of these seven clergy and it allows them to interpret Biblical stories, their own stories, and the stories of others in a way which is graceful and genuinely redemptive. Time and time again, one hears in these sermons the theme that life is worth living in and through the pain, risk, anxiety, and sin which are always part of it. Time and time again, one hears in these sermons that we can genuinely touch each other and help each other because God is real and present in and through our experiences with each other.

This is the Incarnational confession, a theological content which informs all this preaching. It does not answer all questions of life; indeed, it answers none at all. It does provide a grid against which to ask questions, seek the answers, and have the power and the will to act on what seem to be the best answers at any given time. Thus in the end, this is a theology of freedom. It proclaims that we are free to be human, to do the best we can, and leave the rest to God.

A PRESENTATION OF CONTEMPORARY SERMONS

When we first began to talk about putting this book together, several of the contributors were reluctant because they felt strongly that a sermon is an oral event which happens among people within the context of worship. They understood themselves to be in a pastoral relationship with the people to whom they preached, and associated the Holy Spirit with the milieu of a gathered, sacramental community. In fact, not one of us disagreed with this at all. Yet, some of us maintained that the written word is something of a miracle in itself. The Bible is the sedimented product of thousands of years of experience of gathered, sacramental communities and its texts continue to be inexhaustible sources of life for us. So we decided that we could, in good conscience, put sermons into print. At the same time, it seemed a particularly good idea to give each preacher a chance to introduce herself so the reader might have at least a glimpse of the person who preached the sermon. Thus each woman introduces herself with a short self-portrait and prefaces each sermon with a short introduction suggesting her methods and procedures in doing the sermon. Because these introductions are impressionistic and personal, we have included data-based biographies at the end of the book. The sermons have been arranged alphabetically by the preachers' names.

We offer the words of seven women who seek to serve the Word.

The Reverend Charles D. Hackett
Candler School of Theology
Emory University

The Reverend Janice M. Bracken

B aptized into the Body of Christ as an infant, I have always considered the Episcopal Church my home, its members my family. I participated in all the traditional activities of a small suburban parish and thrived on the relationships, the community I found there.

A succession of rectors and curates, many of them young and fresh from seminary, encouraged me to explore a variety of ministries within the church. I participated in the liturgy as a lay reader and chalice bearer for nine years, the first female and the youngest member to serve in this capacity in my home parish. I accompanied the clergy on hospital calls and home visitations. And, in time, I entered the University of Virginia to pursue a degree in religious studies with the hope of developing a ministry of teaching.

My advisor at the university, a brilliant and sensitive Jesuit priest, helped me explore my vocational goals more thoroughly. As he supported my ambition to teach, he also encouraged me to express a deeper calling — a calling to priesthood — an unlikely, if not unattainable calling in 1975.

Three years later, still questioning, still wondering, I entered the Candler School of Theology as a Postulant for Holy Orders from the Diocese of Virginia. There, new ideas and new relationships shaped my theology and my ministry.

Liturgical theology, pastoral care, and homiletics; the excitement of reading, writing, and listening; the variety of denominations represented by the faculty and students — all these things opened my eyes to a concept of church beyond my own limited experience. From an interdenominational seminary to an interracial, international parish placement, my experience of the church grew and my sense of calling to the ordained ministry deepened.

In July of 1981 I was ordained deacon in the Episcopal Church. In June of 1982 I was ordained priest. I see these ordinations not as the end of the process, but as the beginning. In a gracious outpouring of his Holy Spirit, God made me a priest. Exploring, experiencing, and understanding this priesthood is a lifelong process.

Three primary roles come to mind as I consider my life as an ordained minister — prophet, priest, and shepherd.

As prophet, I am called to speak the Word of God for his people today. The prophet is primarily a voice, a messenger standing on the boundary between God and God's people, facing the people and speaking the message. In this role I am called to study and converse with the scripture as I prepare to preach the Word. Preaching is a crucial part of my parish ministry, preaching with insight and sensitivity.

Each sermon becomes a journey for preacher and listener. Sharing the Word means traveling together. Where does the Holy Scripture meet us in a meaningful way today? Where will it change our life and leave its indelible mark?

I cannot pretend to have all the answers; I enjoy raising a variety of questions within the context of the preaching event. For me, creative preaching requires the active participation of both preacher and listener.

I do not attempt to reach my own conclusions about a text and then force these conclusions on my listeners point by point. I prefer to share the process of encountering the text, so that we may experience together the close ties of the gospel story to our own life stories. Each person is then allowed to carry the message through to its conclusion.

The prophet must know when to speak and when to be silent. As preaching grows out of pastoral relationships, the call to listen is every bit as strong as the call to preach. For it is in listening to other people that I come to understand what is important to them. And it is in listening for God that I understand what it is that I am commissioned to say.

While the prophet faces the people with the Word of God, the priest faces God with the petitions and prayers of the people. As priest I serve as a representative before God – the embodiment of the concerns of his people. I am also a channel of God's grace and, by that grace, a steward of the mysteries, the sacraments.

As a woman, I represent men and women at the altar in a way that many have not experienced before. Perhaps my priesthood speaks of the feminine qualities of God's love. More especially, I would hope that the ministry of women brings balance and harmony to the priestly order, reflecting the fullness of God's nature as it is revealed to us.

As shepherd, I am called to stand in the midst of the people, to be a part of the life of my congregation, yet apart from them when objectivity is needed. I am called to guide, to instruct, and to comfort. I become both leader and facilitator, seeking to enable others to develop their own unique ministries.

The roles of prophet, priest, and shepherd are not masks to be worn on the appropriate occasions. They are complex, interrelated responsibilities that accompany the gift of ordination. My response to that gift is thankfulness. And it is my hope that I may express that thankfulness in all aspects of my life and work as an ordained minister, in my relationship with God and with his people.

ADVENT III
Isaiah 35:1-10
Matthew 11:2-11

December 11, 1983
St. Peter's Church
Rome, Georgia

Advent 1983 was indeed a season of preparation, expectation, and commitment for the members of St. Peter's Episcopal Church, Rome, Georgia. Building on the successful ecumenical ministry of the FISH program, which provides food, clothing, and medicine to persons in need, volunteers proposed that we convert an area in one of our buildings into a night shelter for indigent men. The congregation would respond to this challenge at the annual parish meeting on December 13. As I prepared my sermon for Sunday, December 11, the Biblical references to the signs of the Messiah's presence in the world seemed particularly important. Wherever suffering is relieved, we will experience the Lord's presence. It seemed to be a message meant especially for us as we prepared for Christmas. Using the story of an Advent adventure I experienced with young members of the congregation, I presented the gospel message in the context of a situation so similar to our own. How best might we prepare for Christmas? The old traditions still possess their magic and their charm, but perhaps there might be a new way to commit ourselves to the Christ Child, to experience his presence in the world.

The Shar Pei is a rare and centuries-old Chinese fighting dog. Bred for ferocious appearance and feisty temperament, these dogs were trained to fight one another in pit arenas. Grey-brown in color with short, prickly fur, at first glance these dogs look like a mass of wrinkles with legs. Wrinkles and skin everywhere — so ugly, they're cute. And now, in this country, they are in high demand as pets.

Therefore it is not surprising that the Shar Pei heads up the list of Christmas gifts for the "person who has everything." For a mere $2000, Neiman-Marcus will provide you with your own Shar Pei puppy this Christmas.

Just one example of the extravagances and eccentricities that beset us at Christmas time. But if I take this sort of commercial hype with a grain of salt, there can still be a certain magic and excitement to this pre-Christmas season. The plotting and the planning, the shopping and the wrapping, even the last minute rush.

It's in the air . . . and then it hits me . . . it's time to go to Atlanta.

There's a mystique about Atlanta, and perhaps all big cities, at Christmas time, and I'm drawn to it.

I admit that my heart jumps a little when I catch my first glimpse of Rich's department store at Lenox Square decked out for the holiday season, or Davison's, or even Neiman-Marcus.

I feel compelled to take the MARTA train to Rich's downtown store. I want to see Santa, and I want to see the children seeing Santa, and I want to remember the trek to visit Santa that was always a part of my childhood Christmas preparations. I want to be just a little sentimental, to marvel at the huge live tree suspended high over the street below. And I want to see the Pink Pigs "flying" by on the roof at Rich's.

There's something marvelous about the twinkling lights on Peachtree Street. Even the traffic lights sparkle with red and green. And there's something grand about the elegant homes along West Paces Ferry Road with single candles in each window and Della Robbia wreaths.

It's all part of the magic and wonder of getting ready for Christmas. It's a mood. It's a feeling. And, all things considered, it feels very good.

A week ago, 28 of us from St. Peter's made a pre-Christmas pilgrimage to Atlanta; and though it was not intended to be, that trip became an important part of my preparations for Christmas. About 60 of us in all, teenagers and advisors from St. Peter's, Rome, and St. Luke's, Atlanta, boarded a chartered MARTA bus for an all-night tour of the city. We would see another side of the city — many things that we had never seen before. And whether or not we were aware of it, we would be changed by what we saw.

Just blocks away from the sparkling holiday lights of Peachtree Street, we found ourselves dashing through the rain into Grady Hospital. Just minutes from the holiday extravagances of Davison's and Rich's, we were in a barren place — tile walls, tile floors, tile ceilings. We filed past offices and labs, into the emergency area where ambulances arrived and departed without alarm. Accident victims were wheeled past us. Occasionally someone behind the doors of the treatment rooms would shout, or curse, or cry. And there were so many people waiting . . . waiting with blank expressions. It was difficult to tell *what* they were waiting for . . . or whom.

A hospital is an eerie place in the middle of the night . . . especially as you wander past the morgue . . . and feel the chill of the refrigeration units. Nurses and technicians hurried past us as though we weren't there, heading *home* for the night, or someplace.

The chaplain talked with our group for a while, in the warm and lavishly appointed chapel. And he spoke of the people, thousands and thousands of people, who are served by Grady Hospital, in-patient and out-patient. I marvelled at the number of people who could pass through a place in one day . . . *so many* sick people . . . some treated and some sent away.

Then he told us about those who "hide" at Grady. Of the perhaps 4000 street people in Atlanta, many find shelter in the corridors, waiting rooms, and stairwells of Grady. They walk the streets by night and blend into the crowds by day, sleeping in waiting room chairs or propped against a wall in an out-of-the-way space. These people know how to beat the system. They know exactly where "security" won't find them. And they know when to come and go. For hundreds of poor and homeless people, Grady Hospital is "home."

It made me feel sad . . . and a little angry. Why didn't someone do something about a situation like that? It was too painful to think about for very long. After all, I was a visitor, a guest. I didn't live in Atlanta anymore, and it was not my responsibility. I did not want to feel depressed about it; that just wasn't the "Christmas Spirit." But, then I wondered about Christmas without a home.

Back to the bus. The temperatures had dropped and now the rain was pouring. As the driver braved the slick and narrow streets, we travelled past old buildings, stores, and houses. At any given point we were within minutes of the Omni and the Peachtree Plaza, the Hilton and the Hyatt . . . and within minutes of houses without Christmas lights, without heat, without rugs, without food.

Next stop — the City Jail — and a two hour tour at 2:00 in the morning that revealed yet another side of the city. It was a relatively clean place, a new jail, and for a jail, it was as pleasant as you could expect. But it, too, was a barren place — white walls, tile floors, stainless steel — built like a *maze*, we were told, to *confuse* would-be escapees.

In an empty wing we tried out the cells and read the graffiti. It was hot and it was quiet.

But down in the admitting section, it was far from quiet. The shouting and the banging on the walls of the holding cells — the curses and obscenities — all part of the routine — the drunks, the drug addicts, the traffic violators, and even the transvestite in purple leotards — all contributed to the air of unreality. It was a lot like television.

And I didn't worry too much about those people until we came to the maximum security cells, cells without anything, not even a mattress. These were for potential suicides. If our guard said it once, he said it ten times. They had to take every precaution to prevent suicides; it was *not* uncommon.

And I thought about how sad that was — so many people so sick, in mind or spirit, so depressed or so despondent that they would try to take their own lives. The guards really seemed to care, which surprised me. But who else cared? Were there visitors for those people? Could anyone do anything?

But again, it was not my responsibility. I was only a visitor, a guest. I didn't live in Atlanta anymore. If I let it bother me, it would only dampen "the Christmas Spirit." And yet I wondered about being in jail on Christmas.

Back at St. Luke's, at 7:00 in the morning, trying to fix breakfast for the bleary-eyed group. The advisors stumbled around in the quiet kitchen, a kitchen which *explodes* with activity five days a week, feeding 500 people a day in a two-hour time span. Soup and sandwiches, milk and coffee, a place to eat and to get out of the cold. Five hundred hungry people a day passing through for a hot meal. Someone was doing something about a serious problem. I could be glad about that. Even as a visitor, a guest, I could be happy that 500 hungry people had a place to go for a good meal, Monday through Friday, every week of the year. But then, I wondered what it would be like to be hungry on Sunday, what it would be like to be hungry on Christmas.

As we made our way out of the city and onto the interstate, I knew I would return to Atlanta in just a week, to go Christmas shopping and to make my annual pilgrimage to Rich's downtown. With 12 sleeping teenagers sprawled all over the seats of the van, I had plenty of time to think on the way home.

I began to think about what my family and friends would want for Christmas. I smiled as I thought about the piles of ribbons and wrappings that would be scattered around the living room floor back home on Christmas night.

But in my exhausted state, I also wondered for a moment about Christmas. It was Christ's birthday after all. Isn't it strange that *we* receive the gifts? And I pondered what Christ might want for Christmas . . . what I might give him? How I might know his presence on his special day? How would I know he was there?

Isaiah says we will recognize "God with us" when the eyes of the blind are opened, and the ears of the deaf unstopped; when the lame man leaps, and the man who could not speak sings with joy; when sorrow and sighing have fled away.

John the Baptist asked about the presence of the Messiah — and Jesus answered that in His presence, the blind see, and the lame walk, the sick are made well, and the deaf hear. And good news is shared with the poor.

Maybe that is why the "other side" of Atlanta spoke to me about Christmas. Because if we are to believe these passages from the Old and New Testaments, then where the sick are healed, the hungry fed, and the homeless sheltered, THERE we will find the Lord.

When the congregation is new and the pulpit unfamiliar, the challenge of preaching takes on a new dimension. How do I communicate the gospel to a crowd of strangers in a way that will elicit their trust and encourage them to participate in the sermon, the text, and the season? The manuscript which follows was prepared in March of 1984 for the "Lenten New Preacher Series" at All Saints' Episcopal Church, Atlanta, Georgia. Considering the Lenten themes of repentance, forgiveness, and acceptance, I selected as my text Luke 15: 1-7 because of its rich and powerful imagery — the lost sheep and the faithful shepherd. Sharing the story of a personal life experience that made the parable come alive for me in contemporary terms seemed a natural way to invite this congregation to participate in the gospel message.

When I was a very little girl, I cuddled up in my mother's lap and for no apparent reason announced to her that I "knew where I had come from," that I knew how I had come to be *her* little girl. Experiencing a moment of motherly panic over what possible bits of misinformation I could have acquired at such a tender age, my mother took a deep breath and asked with genuine concern, "Well, how *did* you come to be my little girl?"

And with all sincerity I told her my story. The image is still vivid in my mind. I told her that before I was born I was playing in a big field with lots of other children, and that one day Jesus reached over the fence, scooped me up, and sent me to be her little girl.

Relieved, yet somewhat puzzled, my mother didn't say much in response. She just held me tight and I felt very safe and very much loved.

It seems that from these very earliest recollections I wanted to be Jesus' little lamb, that somehow I knew that true security and happiness would be mine if he were holding me. There was a Good Shepherd window in the church where I grew up and I always longed to be the lamb in the Shepherd's arms. To me, that lamb was the happiest and safest, the BEST lamb of all.

In my child's eye, I HAD BEEN Jesus's lamb, and he had held me but then he sent me into a strange new world on the other side of the fence. How was I ever going to be "good enough" for him to hold me again? Thoughts of the little lamb were both comforting, and anxious.

The need to be "good enough" haunted me throughout my youth and adolescence — through 12 years of a church-sponsored school and 12 years of Sunday School. And I was a "good" child, sickeningly good at times! Good grades, good behavior, nice friends, acceptable activities — unnaturally good. But always anxious, always fearing that my best would not be good enough. And if it might not be good enough for my teachers or my parents, I knew that it would not be good enough for God.

And when it came down to the basics of my child-like view of "judgment," it occurred to me that I might become a GOAT and not a SHEEP at all! The ANXIETY heightened.

Then came the college years — they were good. I was good, except of course, when I was just a bit "bad." I trusted God somehow to understand that this was "U. Va." — Cavalier Country — and one couldn't ALWAYS be good! I wasn't ever TERRIBLY bad. And to make matters worse, the people I depended on for feedback were not around. How could I measure up, determine how good or bad I was, if my parents were halfway across the state and my professors weren't overly concerned about the "goodness" of one of their hundreds of students? It didn't take me long before I could add a feeling of isolation and a measure of guilt to the feelings of anxiety. For sanity's sake, I chose to ignore these feelings most of the time and just move ahead with a relatively normal and reasonably happy life.

There followed three good years of seminary. Not only did I love my work and studies, the professional evaluations tended to report that I was "good" at what I was doing. That FELT good. But there was always a nagging doubt — was it "good" enough? What about the times when nothing tangible, nothing obviously positive, came out of hours of effort and work? Why didn't people always respond to my teaching or preaching or counseling? Wasn't it "good" enough for them?

And so, added to the anxiety and the isolation and the guilt, there was anger, subtle and diffuse, but anger just the same. Again, most often, I chose to ignore these feelings, and go on.

Over the next few years I came across my share of old goats and lost sheep. And then there was Sarah. I met Sarah in a hospital where I was assigned to be her counselor and confessor. If ever there was a truly lost sheep, it was Sarah. That was obvious from the start, so obvious it was scary. And Sarah knew it.

During the hours we spent together, Sarah described her life, all 22 years of it. It had been for her a "bad" life. She had been a "bad" girl and now she felt "bad" about it.

The stories were gruesome. Sarah had been born "out of wedlock." Her mother never really wanted her and did everything she could to let her know that. Sarah had been a battered child, bounced from this foster home to that, occasionally landing back with her natural mother; but that never lasted very long.

At an early age, Sarah experimented with illegal drugs. They were fun at first, an escape. But soon they became a necessity, a burden. Sarah spent so much time "in the streets" that she quickly learned the so-called easy ways to make money. By the time she was 16, she was working as a prostitute.

It sounded too terrible to be true; but it was true. Sarah was really that bad. She had stolen, she had lied, she had run away. Who knows what else she had done that she didn't tell me! I always did my best not to look horrified when she talked to me. But the feelings inside me were so intense — shock, pity, disbelief.

And Sarah *knew* how bad she was. In fact, she hated herself most of the time, for what she had done and for what she had become, worthless in her own eyes. Now she was hospitalized, trying to break a drug habit, and searching for a way out of her "bad" situation.

She spoke to me one afternoon, "I know I'm going to hell. And I'm afraid. I've read some of the Bible and I've heard the preachers. I *know* I'm going to hell. I've been so BAD that God won't *ever* forgive me. How could he forgive me? I'm so sorry. He'll never forgive me when I've been this bad."

As I looked at her, I saw the total despair in her eyes and I knew she was one lost sheep that didn't want to be lost anymore. I virtually exploded with what I knew in faith and what I so desperately wanted her to experience with me.

"He WILL forgive you! I don't care how bad you think you've been — he will forgive you. God is great enough to forgive and to love every one of us. Keep reading your Bible, Sarah; Jesus didn't die on the cross for us because we were so GOOD, but because we were so BAD! He loved everyone — but especially the people who had problems. He loved the prostitutes and the thieves, and people made fun of him and criticized him because he loved the people they thought were "bad." But he forgave all their faults when they followed him."

It was a frantic time. I wanted so much to tell her ALL the Good News! I could have told her about Paul. How much worse could you be than Paul, the persecutor of Christians, and Jesus forgave him and made him an apostle! I could have told her about the shady tax collectors and the thief on the cross, and Mary Magdalene. Jesus forgave all of them when they followed him. They just asked, that's all. They said they knew they had been estranged from God by their actions and lifestyles, and they ASKED for forgiveness. And he forgave them! For things done and things left undone, he forgave them and he loved them.

But that certainly wasn't the time for such a drawn out exposition of the New Testament. For a fleeting moment, Sarah had perceived in our relationship something about acceptance and forgiveness, and there were tears in her eyes. We hugged each other. And as we held each other, we BOTH cried.

It was only in that crisis situation that I could blurt out what I really believed about forgiveness. For once, it rang perfectly true and I experienced a feeling of release and relief . . . because Sarah was not the only LOST SHEEP in that room! She was not the only one who needed to experience acceptance and forgiveness. As we held each other, we were both lost sheep that had been found. Through our reaching out to one another, Jesus had indeed found us. And all we had to do was listen to his Good News, and believe it! How incredible that two people could embody that Good News for each other! He was holding us.

In all the time that I had been trying so hard to be "good" and "acceptable," longing for the Lord to love me and hold me, I had wandered farther and farther away. Like the sheep nibbling its way away from the flock, moving thoughtlessly from this tuft of grass to that, through this hole in the fence into the thicket, I had strayed from the flock and the shepherd, allowing feelings of anxiety and isolation and guilt and anger to block my own hearing of Jesus' words — his promise of love and forgiveness.

It had taken me so long to realize that the little lamb the Good Shepherd is holding is NOT the "good" sheep, the best lamb. Instead, it is the sheep who wandered off, the sheep the shepherd was willing to leave the 99 to search for, the sheep who had been lost and now was found.

How incredible that he searches for us all along. How remarkable that he longs to hold us as much as we need to be held.

PENTECOST VI
Matthew 13:24-30, 36-43

July 22, 1984
St. Peter's Church
Rome, Georgia

The Bible is a rich anthology of poetry and prose. Biblical texts range in form from hymn to epistle, from narrative to discourse, from proverb to parable. If we insist upon preaching every sermon in the same narrative or didactic style, we may be missing important opportunities to respond to the "form" of the text. On occasion, the medium becomes the message. The gospel selection for July 22, 1984 — Matthew 13:2-30, 36-43 — included two distinct literary forms: a parable of Jesus, and an explanation of that parable, an allegory. At first I felt frustrated that the author of the Gospel of Matthew would "ruin" the parable of the weeds by assigning an allegorical interpretation. But then I realized that the allegory contained a message and a meaning of its own. The sermon which follows combines the shape of an allegory with the message of the gospel text — unconventional, but effective.

In the beginning God created the heavens and the earth, everything *in* the heavens and *on* the earth. And when God saw everything that he had made; behold, it was very good.

In the beginning, God made that Judgment; and the Judgment said that creation was very good. And so a Good Judgment came into being.

God pondered this new creature — Good Judgment — and decided that this, too, should be entrusted to the care of human beings. Good Judgment seemed full of hope and promise, an appropriate gift for man and woman.

And so, when God instructed Adam and Eve in the care and feeding of the birds of the air and the beasts of the field, he also told them about Good Judgment.

"If you care for Good Judgment and feed him regularly, your Good Judgment will grow and become stronger. "Most importantly," God reminded them, "you must never forget to *exercise* Good Judgment. If you do not *exercise* Good Judgment, Good Judgment will leave you altogether, just when you need Good Judgment the most."

"Is Good Judgment one of a kind?" Eve asked.

"No," God answered with some hesitation. "There are other Judgments, and you will meet them, too, someday."

"Name one!" Adam prodded.

"There is Final Judgment," God replied.

"May we meet Final Judgment now? May we have Final Judgment, too?"

"No," said the Lord God. "I have given you Good Judgment, and that is the only Judgment I intend for you to have today. So go and exercise Good Judgment as I have instructed you. Final Judgment is mine, and mine alone."

Time passed in the Garden of Eden. At first Adam and Eve were very faithful in exercising Good Judgment every day. But one day Adam and Eve felt bored and restless; they did not take the time or make the effort to exercise Good Judgment that day. Good Judgment was neglected and slipped away from them.

When a certain snake in a forbidden tree noticed that Good Judgment had wandered away, he seized the opportunity to introduce God's people to a Judgment they did not know — Bad Judgment.

The snake wove a grand and glorious tale about the care and feeding of Bad Judgment, assuring Adam and Eve that exercising Bad Judgment would be far easier than exercising Good Judgment — that it would take less effort, less attention, and certainly, less commitment.

Adam and Eve believed the scaly devil and, in doing so, began exercising Bad Judgment right away.

God was sorely disappointed that Adam and Eve had chosen to exercise Bad Judgment. But as he sent them out of the Garden in punishment, he again encouraged them lovingly to exercise the Good Judgment he had given them, to allow Good Judgment to go with them wherever they went.

"It seems you must now take Bad Judgment with you, too," God sighed, "but I warn you to keep Bad Judgment in a strong muzzle and on a short leash . . ."

"What about Final Judgment," his people asked him. "Do we meet Final Judgment now?"

"No, it is not time," God replied. "And remember, Final Judgment, is mine, and mine alone."

Over the centuries, men and women continued to respond to God's challenge to exercise Good Judgment and to keep Bad Judgment under lock and key. Historians recorded the details.

Certain famous figures fared better than others in the annals of history. Sad to say, events involving Bad Judgment were often far more memorable.

King David, for example, was a great soldier and faithful leader of God's people — most of the time. But there came a day when Bad Judgment came into play. Bad Judgment teased and tempted David to play with him.

It seems there was a beautiful woman named Bathsheba, and David wanted her for himself. But he knew that she was married to one of the most loyal officers of the army, Uriah the Hittite.

Bad Judgment told David that plotting the death of Uriah would solve this problem. If Uriah were dead, David could have Bathsheba.

And so, David gave in to the temptation and exercised Bad Judgment. He made the choice to have Uriah killed.

God was very angry with David. He punished David for exercising Bad Judgment. "How dare you cause the death of an innocent man? You have overstepped your bounds!" God roared.

How many, throughout history, would overstep their bounds by exercising Bad Judgment? So many . . . Too many . . .

And to make matters worse, Bad Judgment could NEVER be trusted! Bad Judgment often took delight in masquerading as Final Judgment. Men and women were fooled into thinking that THEY were exercising Final Judgment — the Judgment they did not know — when, in fact, they were only exercising Bad Judgment all along. God's people forgot that Final Judgment belonged to God, and God alone.

Over time, Bad Judgment led more and more people to think that they were better than other people — by reason of birth, or skill, or color, or education, or nationality, or position, or wealth, or creed.

Deluded, by Bad Judgment, into thinking that they should ACT on this belief, many, many people decided to "improve" their world by subordinating or even eliminating those they thought to be inferior, or unworthy, or evil . . .

They struggled to create their own Final Judgment. And there was slavery and oppression . . . anger, prejudice and murder . . . war and destruction . . . political prisoners . . . religious prisoners . . . prisoners of war . . . there were Crusades and Inquisitions . . . there was the Holocaust and there was Jonestown . . . and long, long ago, there was a torchlit garden, a crown of thorns, a bloody cross, and a borrowed grave. Human beings clamoring to have the final word.

"We are protecting the good and destroying what is evil!" the crusaders of every generation cried.

But God could only shake his head and plead again with his wayward children. "You cannot overcome the evil in this world alone. Good Judgment will tell you that. To think that you can is sheer folly and arrogance. You cannot have the final word, though you behave as if you do.

STOP! And allow Good Judgment to show you that you may be doing far more harm that good.

"But we are weeding out the world for you, Lord — and we're working hard at it!" the faithful crusaders pleaded again.

"Always work hard, my children," the Lord God replied, "but work hard at the tasks I have given you from the beginning — caring for creation and exercising Good Judgment. Trust me to take care of the rest. I have entrusted Good Judgment into your care. But remember, Final Judgment is mine, and mine alone," said the Lord.

He who has ears, let him hear.

The Reverend Eloise Hally

I came to ministry by way of a long sojourn in the secular world: Peace Corps teacher, 60s dropout, Washington government worker, graduate student, and teacher of economics. In my itinerant, military family childhood, both the Catholic faith of my father and the Congregational church of my mother were significant influences. But I left the church for what I thought were areas excluded from religion — the intellectual vistas opened up by my years at Vassar College. I did not make a serious adult re-examination of Christianity until I passed the age of 30. By then I had married, settled in Atlanta, had a child, and was in the midst of an identity crisis of sorts. The good news, the excitement, the relief, and the peace and grace of finding that sojourner — myself — in the Biblical stories are much of what I bring to preaching.

Preaching, or rather the preparation and writing of sermons, is the crucible in which my theology is formed and articulated. In coming to grips with a Biblical text, I see where I stand on a theological issue. Sometimes in that process, and this is always my hope, God reveals another place to stand. I also always hope that some of my love and respect for the Biblical text will be conveyed to the hearers. In a time when authority is either suspect or slavishly obeyed, serious dialogue with the Bible offers another way to relate to the sourcebook of our faith.

Besides a love for the Bible, I bring to preaching a strong interest in pastoral care and counseling. Because so much of my own early hearing of the gospel came in a pastoral counseling relationship, it is almost natural to listen to Biblical conversations with the third ear. Guarding against psychologizing the Bible is, therefore, especially important.

Searching for the hermeneutical bridge from Bible to congregation is particularly exciting in the Episcopal congregations of urban and suburban Atlanta. Their members are highly educated, psychologically sophisticated, and acutely interested in the gospel for their lives. The most difficult and challenging aspect of the preaching endeavor in this setting is conveying the social, corporate nature of salvation — how it can be good news for the rich to serve the neighbor. This challenge remains open for me for the future.

The corporate dimension is also important for me in the preaching of a sermon. Preaching is an act of worship, and worship, especially in the Anglican tradition, is a corporate event. Most of the sermons I preach are in the context of a Sunday morning Eucharist, where the culmination of worship is the Holy Communion. The service opens with prayers and hymns; three lessons from the lectionary are read and the sermon is preached, fairly early in the order of worship. In the sermon, I try to point, in one way or another, to the corporate sacrament of shared remembrance, grace, and hope.

LENT III
John 4:5-26, 39-42

March 9, 1983
All Saints' Church
Atlanta, Georgia

All Saints' Church is a sophisticated downtown Atlanta congregation. I was visiting preacher at a mid-week Lenten preaching service and chose this text from the weekdays of Lent lectionary with the Lenten theme of self-examination in the back of my mind. I also felt that an All Saints' Lenten congregation might be willing to grapple with what to me is a very difficult passage from the gospel of John. I began with my own puzzlements about the text. And, in a crazy kind of dialogue with the text about my own questions, the Good News emerged.

The framers of the lectionary for the weekdays of Lent have chosen for us one of the longest conversations Jesus has with anybody in the Bible:

So he came to a city of Samaria, called Sychar, near the field that Jacob gave to his son Joseph. Jacob's well was there, and so Jesus, wearied as he was with his journey, sat down beside the well. It was about the sixth hour.

There came a woman of Samaria to draw water. Jesus said to her, "Give me a drink." For his disciples had gone away into the city to buy food. The Samaritan woman said to him, "How is it that you, a Jew, ask a drink of me, a woman of Samaria?" For Jews have no dealings with Samaritans. Jesus answered her, "If you knew the gift of God, and who it is that is saying to you, 'Give me a drink,' you would have asked him, and he would have given you living water." The woman said to him, "Sir, you have nothing to draw with, and the well is deep; where do you get that living water? Are you greater than our father Jacob, who gave us the well, and drank from it himself, and his sons, and his cattle?" Jesus said to her, "Everyone who drinks of this water will thirst again, but whoever drinks of the water that I shall give him will never thirst; the water that I shall give him will become in him a spring of water welling up to eternal life." The woman said to him, "Sir, give me this water, that I may not thirst, nor come here to draw."

Jesus said to her, "Go, call your husband, and come here." The woman answered him, "I have no husband." Jesus said to her, "You are right in saying, 'I have no husband'; for you have had five husbands, and he whom you now have is not your husband; this you said truly." The woman said to him, "Sir, I perceive that you are a prophet. Our fathers worshiped on this mountain; and you say that in Jerusalem is the place where men ought to worship."

Jesus said to her, "Woman, believe me, the hour is coming when neither on this mountain nor in Jerusalem will you worship the Father. You worship what you do not know, we worship what we know, for salvation is from the Jews. But the hour is coming, and now is, when the true worshippers will worship the Father in spirit and truth, for such the Father seeks to worship him. God is spirit, and those who worship him must worship in spirit and truth." The woman said to him, "I know that Messiah is coming (he who is called Christ); when he comes, he will show us all things." Jesus said to her, "I who speak to you am He."

Many Samaritans from that city believed in him because of the woman's testimony, "He told me all that I ever did." So when the Samaritans came to him, they asked him to stay with them; and he stayed there two days. And many more believed because of his word. They said to the woman, "It is no longer because of your words that we believe, for we have heard for ourselves, and we know that this is indeed the Savior of the world."

Not only is this a long conversation, but to my mind, it's one of the hardest to really get a hold of. It's hard to follow: Jesus and the woman seem to go from one topic to another very abruptly, with no transitions. It's like the bishop told me once about one of my sermons; he said, "Eloise, you need to double-clutch your transitions."

Their conversation starts with a simple request by a tired traveler for a drink of water, but we are very soon into a discussion of living water and where that might come from, Jacob's well and who is greater, Jacob or Jesus, the woman's marital history, Samaritan vs. Jewish worship, true spiritual worship and then, Jesus' declaration that he is the Messiah. He says: "The one who is speaking to you — I AM."

After their conversation, she goes into town to call the people to see a man who told her all she ever did. That seems to me to be a rather strange way to sum up a conversation with the Messiah, the Incarnate God. Because that final response of hers struck me as so strange I want to focus on their conversation — to try to see why she left her encounter with Jesus saying: "He told me all that I ever did."

Why is that Good News? To her — and to us? Now, one of the most noticeable things about their conversation is that Jesus and the woman seem to be on different wave lengths:

She says: "How is that you, a Jew, ask a drink of me, a woman of Samaria?" and he replies: "If you knew who I am, you'd be asking me for living water."

So she says: "With no bucket, where do get this living water?" and He replies: "If you drink this living water, you will never thirst again."

These two people are NOT on the same wave length.

These kinds of conversations are fairly typical of the gospel of John. In the chapter right before the Samaritan story, Nicodemus has his famous conversation with Jesus about being born again.

Jesus says: "Unless one is born anew, he cannot see the Kingdom of God."
Nicodemus protests: "How can a man be born when he is old? Can he enter a second time into his mother's womb and be born?"

John uses these conversations to show us something about the levels of our existence — about our denseness over the depth of our encounters.

The Samaritan woman and Jesus are having their conversation on *two different levels;* you might say hers is a literal level and his a symbolic, or that she's dealing with what's going on in the here and now, and he's talking about what's *really* going on in the here and ever after. She's resisting an encounter with who he might really be. He's talking on the level of identity and relationship.

I've been in some of those two-level conversations. With me, they usually start on a literal level, level one. Level two has to do with the relationship.

I remember telling a dream I had about soldiers and guns, telling it rather naively, without much sense of its meaning, early on in a counseling relationship,

"It was awful," I said on level one, "there were soldiers, guards with guns, underground guards like in resistance movements during the war."
The counselor said, on level two: "I'm not afraid of your guns; you don't scare me."
"Oh," I said. And pondered a good while over that.

Or another conversation between friends:

Level one: He — I hate it when you're late — I hate rushing to a movie.
She — We have enough time — we can make it.
Level two: He — Actually, it's the insecurity I hate, wondering if you have mixed feelings about being with me.
She — Well, I was feeling a bit pressed into going to this movie, but I was afraid to say I didn't want to go.

There's something freeing about both people getting to the level of what's going on in the relationship, of talking about who they are to each other.

It happened with my daughter, age 7, and a friend the other day. She came to me in tears, saying:

"Mama, Jennifer doesn't want to play with the Barbie dolls. She *said* she wanted to, so I got them out and all set up and now she doesn't want to."
Jennifer came in saying: "I want to play the Smurf Game."
Claire — more tears: "Well, why did you say you'd play Barbie dolls?"
Jennifer — "I don't know."

Claire to me: "I feel like she doesn't like me."
Jennifer: "Yes, I do. I like you. I just saw the Smurf Game and wanted to
    play it."
Claire: "Well, okay, maybe we can play both."
Jennifer: "Yeah. Okay."

In the gospel of John, who Jesus is to the people he encounters, and how they
stand in relationship to each other is all important. What matters is on the second, deeper level. "One who believes in the Son has eternal life," writes John,
just before the story of the Samaritan woman.

This deep level focus is there on Jesus' part right from the beginning in the
conversation with the Samaritan woman. He already knows who she is to him.
The important thing for him is his identity to her and the gift he has for her.
Remember his replies to her first two questions: "If you knew who was asking
you for a drink, you would have asked him for living water," and "Whoever
drinks of the water that I shall give them will never thirst."

But it takes the Samaritan woman a little while to get in deep. It's actually one
of the things I like about her — the touch of skepticism, the breath of everyday
realism she brings to the conversation. She doesn't get into second level conversations too readily with strange men at wells.

It's all very well for Jesus to start talking about eternal life in the second breath
of a conversation, but I can tell you her resistant stance is more how I'd be: "How
is it that you, a Jew, ask a drink of me, a woman of Samaria?" (The Jews taught
that Samaritan women were as menstruants from their cradle — unclean,
unclean!) Remember, too, that this is a woman who has had five husbands. She's
had some experience with men.

It's easy to read in even an edge of scorn or hostility to her tone with Jesus:
"You don't even have a bucket and the well is deep. Where would *you get* that
living water? It was our ancestor Jacob who gave us the well. He and his children
and his flocks all drank from it. You don't claim to be greater than Jacob, do
you?" (John throws in a little irony here.)

But Jesus persists and describes the water that he will give her, the water that
will become a spring inside a person welling up to eternal life. The one who
drinks it will never thirst again. When Jesus makes this offer, she decides to go
ahead and ask for the water — even though she's still not entirely on his wave
length. She says: "Sir, give me this water, that I may not thirst, nor come here to
draw water."

You may remember that it is at this point that Jesus responds with the non-
sequitur: "Go, call your husband, and come here." At least it would be a non-
sequitur in ordinary conversation. But remember Jesus' opening challenge to
her: "If you knew who I AM you would ask me and I would give you living
water."

He tells her at the very beginning what he wants from her. She doesn't quite know who he is (the first part of the challenge), but she takes a chance and asks for the living water, whatever it might be. Up to the end she's still wondering if he's the Messiah, but they're beginning to talk on the same level.

The wonderful thing about the Samaritan woman to me is that she knows she's receiving a gift when she gets it. Somehow she sees his "Go, call your husband" as a gift. She *could* have gone away, back into the darkness, back to the man she called her husband, and never returned. But she chose not to; she chose to come to the light and let her deeds be exposed. She makes a connection between truth and light and living water.

Not everyone received the light, John tells us in the very beginning of the gospel. The Incarnate Word came to his own and his own received him not. Some loved darkness rather than light because their deeds were evil.

It's a harsh, glaring light Jesus brings to her: "You are right in saying, 'I have no husband' for you have had five husbands, and he whom you now have is not your husband; this you said truly." It takes courage to come into the light. The rabbi said more than three marriages was *not okay*. Here's a woman in a seemingly endless cycle of marrying and divorcing, marrying, and divorcing — dieting and gaining weight, going from job to job, doctor to doctor, school to school, group to group, relationship to relationship — an endless cycle of disappointment, anger and frustration.

WHEN IS SHE GOING TO STOP AND DEAL WITH THE ISSUES?

WHEN IS SHE GOING TO STOP RUNNING AND LET THE PAST CATCH UP WITH HER AND TURN AND FACE IT?

The Samaritan woman stopped. She let the past catch up with her when she met Jesus and he gave her the truth about herself as the wellspring of eternal life.

He gave her the truth about herself as the wellspring of eternal life. Her testimony — "he told me all that I ever did" seemed strange at first, but "all that she ever did" — that's her past — she's free of it now. It's been brought to light and she hasn't been destroyed. He's still there with her.

She has control of her past now; it doesn't control her. She can fling it around — use it to call the townspeople to Jesus: "Come, see a man who told me all I ever did."

And they did come — on the strength of her testimony, the witness of a sinner; they went to Jesus to hear for themselves.

After the long prologue of Lent and Holy Week, Easter's "He is risen!" speaks clearly as the climax of the ancient drama. It needs no translation. But, by the Sixth Sunday of Easter, the last of the Easter season, that immediacy has faded. We are no longer at the apex of dramaturgical worship, the Passion Narrative, but are all too quickly back in the secular world. We're no longer part of the events of Jesus' life, but wondering how he fits into ours. The Easter message then needs another kind of prologue to speak to a changed context; Paul, par excellence, spoke to a world outside the events of Holy Week. I realized how strongly I share Paul's passion to evangelize the secular world — especially the secular world within us. While this sermon is much like a lecture, some of my own intense feelings about the quest for meaning, religion, and secular existence must have come through in the delivery.

Sometime after Easter, Paul, the new apostle, began to travel in the Gentile world spreading the Good News of God in Jesus Christ. He made several journeys, with different companions, to various cities of the known world. He and his friends usually headed straight for the local synagogue as the most convenient place to get a hearing for their message. There they would engage the Jews in scriptural arguments and encounter interested Gentiles as well.

Paul's evangelizing produced mixed and often very violent results. Some Jews and leading Greeks usually were converted; others of the Jews and Greeks wanted to run Paul out of town on a rail or on whatever the contemporary equivalent was. More often than not, Paul's evangelizing set a whole town in an uproar; often there were demonstrations and lynch mobs and the police were called in. If Paul did not end up in jail for disturbing the peace and inciting to unlawful behavior, he had to be smuggled out of town to escape lynch mobs. Preaching before a crowd of strangers was more risky in those days.

On the trip we call Paul's second missionary journey, the apostle and his companion Silas had great success among the Thessalonian Jews and their Gentile proselytes. They were so successful that they had to leave Thessalonica by night in the midst of a riot for fear of reprisals. They were smuggled out to Berea, but as soon as they began preaching there, the unconverted Jews from Thessalonica heard about it and came down to Berea to get Paul. Paul was preaching, so they incited the crowd around the synagogue. The converts at Berea had to get Paul out of there in a hurry; a couple of them took him to Athens, leaving Silas and

Timothy in Berea. (Indiana Jones has nothing on Paul in terms of narrow escapes!)

So Paul found himself alone in Athens, waiting for his friends. And his spirit was provoked within him, the Book of Acts tells us, as he saw that the city was full of idols. That's like honey to a bear, for Paul, like a crowd of smokers before an ex-smoker. He had to speak. The hot breath of a lynch mob had barely cooled and he went out to argue in synagogue and in the marketplace with any who happened to be there.

Now Athens, fortunately for Paul's physical health, was rather more tolerant of foreigners than Thessalonica and Berea. You might see anything at the Piedmont Park Arts Festival, but the same thing in Waycross might not go over so well.

Of course, in a sophisticated city like Athens, Paul was just another new speaker. He attracted the attention of the curious, who would be just as interested tomorrow in the *next* new guru. Some of the old established philosophers, the Stoics and the Epicureans, also met with Paul, but they were not impressed. The way the Book of Acts describes the Athenians, they sound like today's readers of pop psychology. One day it's *Games People Play,* then it's Reality Therapy, or *I'm O.K., You're O.K.,* while the old Freudians look on scornfully. How does a Christian get a hearing in that kind of world? How do you talk Christ with people who only *hear* psychology but are obsessed with power, ritual, and symbols?

In Paul's case, it was how do you talk Christ with people who only *hear* the arguments of philosophers but are fully occupied with the rituals of religion?

In any event, the Athenians were sufficiently intrigued by Paul to bring him to speak before the "Aeropagus," a powerful group of citizens who held court on a hill next to the Acropolis. One of the functions of this group was to exercise vigilance over foreigners.

Today's reading from Acts is Paul's speech to the Areopagus: "Men of Athens," he said (and it *was* only men — it seems men didn't work in those days but hung around the public squares a lot). "Men of Athens, I perceive that in every way you are religious. For as I passed along and observed the objects of your worship, I found also an altar with this inscription: 'To an unknown god.' What therefore you worship as unknown, I proclaim to you. The God who made the world and everything in it, being Lord of heaven and earth, does not live in shrines made by human beings, nor is he served by human hands, as though he needed anything, since he himself gives to all life and breath and everything."

See, Paul is talking to the secular world here. He's full of the Easter message, he wants to talk with the people of Athens about God, but he's got to find a way to connect with them in their language. He's got to relate to them an issue that's important to them. He sees that they are religious, they are seekers, that they are so aware of divine power that if they don't know which god to thank or propitiate, they pour out an offering to an unknown god. Paul sees all this religious activity as evidence of the deep hunger and longing of all people to find God — God their creator.

Augustine put it this way: "O God, you made us for yourself and our hearts are restless until we find ourselves in you." Paul says to Athens: "And God made from one person . . . every nation to live on all the face of the earth . . . that they should seek God in the hope that they might feel after him and find him."

Paul has to find a point of common language. It's not like talking to the Jews; they're expecting a Messiah and he has to show them in the Scriptures that the Messiah must suffer and die. Talking to secular Athens is more like talking to modern secular America; no religious Messiah is expected, yet gods are everywhere worshipped. Paul would notice the standard idols of money, prestige, patriotism, fame, physical fitness, social status, education, beauty, talent, inner peace, being liked, being successful, being fulfilled, having a happy family life, etc., etc., and all the rituals which are faithfully observed to obtain the favor of these gods.

Take the god of being liked, for example, and consider the rituals this idol seems to demand: always speaking politely, never getting angry, not asking for what you want, pretending you like everybody, volunteering for all the dirty work, hardly ever saying no, etc. Or the god of success — this idol often demands the sacrifice of family life and real friendships with co-workers. Rituals may involve "dressing for success" and looking the part, long hours, frequent moves, taking promotions you don't want, entertaining people you don't like, and so on.

People of Atlanta, Paul says, I perceive that you are very religious; but no matter how many miles you jog, pounds you lose, health foods you eat, workshops and parenting seminars you attend, you will not find what you seek. For what you seek is reconciliation with yourself and your neighbor — and ultimately that is neither a psychological nor a behavioral question, but the religious quest of all human beings. The religious quest is to seek the ground of our being and the assurance of our creator's care for us.

Paul wants to tell the idolatrous, seeking, yearning world about the love of God in Jesus Christ, but he can't jump in with Jesus talk right away; he has to find a point of contact. He lights on the Greek connection between nature and the divine and he focuses on the relationship of humans and the divine creator.

He chooses two quotes from Greek writers to make his point. Paul says: "God is not far from each one of us, for 'in him we live and move and have our being,' and even as some of your poets have said: 'For we are indeed his offspring.'" And being God's offspring, Paul continues, "We cannot worship that which comes from the human imagination and is represented by the art of human beings."

Paul prizes something very important about the Athenians — they have a sense of the Holy and a sense of their own creatureliness. Yes, their reverence is displaced to idols, but they have a sense of humility before the Divine. Paul sees what is going on in Athens — all that seemingly religious activity — that idol worship is evidence of the Athenians' quest for the Holy in their lives.

He couches his address to them in the issues of their day. Paul knows you can't argue people into the Kingdom of God. In Athens he *didn't* have a mass conversion of the Athenians. At the end of his speech, as he began to talk about resurrection, many mocked him; but others said "We will hear you again about this. But some joined him and believed — among them, Dionysius the Areopagate and a woman named Damaris and others with them." Yes, Paul knows you can't argue people into the Kingdom of God, but he also realizes that sometimes rearranging the mental furniture is necessary so the door can be opened!

Augustine couldn't accept Christianity for years. Then one day he heard Ambrose explain how the Bible didn't have to be interpreted literally. From that point on he grew rapidly in faith.

I remember as a young teenager (nobody told me about the theological significance of the miracle stores), I thought you had to believe Jesus was a magician to be a Christian. I didn't know how to relate science and religion then, and that seemed important — to be able to include my intelligence and experience in religion, even though I couldn't articulate my problem. Once the mental furniture was rearranged, theology was no longer an insult to intellect.

Paul knows that what goes on every day in people's lives has to be included in religion. The worship of idols is not simply a bad behavior to be cut out, but a symptom of being unaware or cut off from the living God and his assurance to us in Jesus Christ.

Paul, I think, wouldn't offer Christianity today as a new psychology, but I think he'd make an effort to meet us on that ground. The religious quest is not *primarily* about lowering our anxiety levels and resolving our internal conflicts, but these are issues of the day and Christianity has to address them to evangelize the secular world.

Perhaps Paul would say to the people of Atlanta, "God embraces your anxiety about not being liked, your loneliness, the parts of you at war with each other and thus at war with your neighbors. These issues and others are taken seriously in the church and aren't met simply with pious platitudes, such as, 'if you had more faith, you wouldn't feel that way.' " Perhaps Paul would also say to the people of Atlanta, "I perceive that in every way you are very religious, you struggle with feelings of emptiness and issues of meaning — you look to the arts and to the sciences for meaning — even one of your art museums is dedicated to the arts as the 'continuing struggle of the human spirit to find meaning in existence!' "

Paul would say that this struggle — the search for meaning — is the search for God. And he would say, as to the Athenians, "What you seek, I proclaim to you, I proclaim the God who meets us in Jesus Christ, and of this, God has given assurance to all by raising Jesus from the dead." Amen.

This is less a sermon than a meditation, a reflection from the Biblical scene, a paraphrasing of "what happened." I began simply to retell the story, starting with setting the scene from a distance and moving, as the story did, closer and closer. I remember thinking about how I would film the scene, beginning with pan shots of the crowd and then to close-ups of the faces on the crosses. The words wrote themselves, as sermons sometimes do.

The Church of the Atonement is a small, intimate congregation, one in which I served for over a year as deacon and newly ordained priest. Our relationship was a close one, the physical setting was intimate (no mike, no high pulpit), and their listening and hearing was intense and open. You had to strain to hear this; it's much easier to read it.

For the Last Sunday After Pentecost, Christ The King, the Gospel reading, Luke 23: 35-43, lets us in on a very unusual throne-room scene:

The people stood by, watching; but the rulers scoffed at him, saying, "He saved others; let him save himself, if he is the Christ of God, his Chosen One!" The soldiers also mocked him, coming up and offering him vinegar, and saying, "If you are the King of the Jews, save yourself!" There was also an inscription over him, "This is the King of the Jews." One of the criminals who was hanged railed at him, saying, "Are you not the Christ? Save yourself and us!" But the other rebuked him, saying, "Do you not fear God, since you are under the same sentence of condemnation? And we indeed justly; for we are receiving the due reward of our deeds; but this man has done nothing wrong." And he said, "Jesus, remember me when you come into your kingdom." And he said to him, "Truly, I say to you, today you will be with me in paradise."

A Conversation Among Three Who Are Dying

Jesus in the middle
a sign over his head
"This is the King of the Jews"
Otherwise, we couldn't tell him
apart from the other two —

They were all dying
They knew they were dying
That's what makes their conversation interesting.
(If interesting is the right word — I think it is.
Although perhaps 'vital' would be better.)

What would three dying people say to each other?
Surely one of the conversations one would be most drawn to overhear.
But intrusive, surely, to eavesdrop on
something so . . . naked, so final:
These three share a fate that shapes their words.
The pressure of the nails on flesh
lifts their tongues and forms their lips.
Those who simply overhear don't
have that pressure to change their hearing.
You have to know you're dying
for ears to hear.

One thing about being on a cross,
it put them above the crowd.
It swirled beneath them, rulers, people, soldiers
mocking, watching:
they still wanted something —
that's what made them angry,
made them wait.
I don't think they mocked the other two,
only despised them.
We know this by the death they gave them.

There were the three, aligned, raised up
above the crowd —
2 embezzlers, 1 pretender
to the throne of God —
But one belongs among the crowd:
he uses their mocking words
"Are you not the Christ? Save yourself,"
he adds, "and us."
The mockers on the ground didn't think
to add "save us."
They didn't feel the pressure of the nails on flesh.
Being under some anesthetic of their own choosing.

He may have used their words, their wishes,
but, don't you know his voice was different,
formed by pain, as I said before,
desperate, scornful, urgent.

Are you not the Christ? Why
let us stay in our agony? Get us down.
A strain of pleading tempers rage.

I wouldn't minimize his pain — I couldn't
but I think he thought the agony would be over
if only he could get down from that cross.
He knew he was dying, all right
but he didn't know he was dying.
He thought being saved meant no more of this pain —
'Save yourself and us' meant do your magic
— if you've got any, do it now, for chrissake —
save us from *this* death, *this* pain, *this* fix.

He didn't have the big picture
the one where
everybody dies
the one where
death shapes life
as well as words.
You have to know you're dying
to live.

But who can blame him;
the pain must have been very great.
Pain can do that — blot out the big picture, I mean.
Life must have been hell before the crucifixion.

The conversation continues
The second speaker speaks
He blames the first —
I guess he can do it because he's hanging there with him
"Do you not fear God, since you are under
the same sentence of condemnation?
And we indeed, justly; for we are receiving
the due reward of our deeds; but
this man has done nothing wrong."

Quite a long speech for a dying man.
He must have spoken with some passion
It must have been something he had to say
— not the rebuke, but the vision behind it —
a vision of justice, finally in focus
obscured by a lifetime
revealed by the suffering of an innocent man.

He could have said it all differently
spoken only of himself, to himself.

After all, why rebuke a dying man?
But remember
this is a three-way conversation.
Speaker One had railed at Jesus
Speaker Two, perhaps for once in his life,
speaks out against injustice.
His rebuke is not so much rebuke
as it is defense of innocence.
Of course, proclaiming Jesus innocent
means seeing himself as sinner,
A small price to pay for a new vision
And, he had choice in this new life —
He could speak or not in defense of Jesus.
You have to know you're dying
for eyes to see
Do you not fear God? Do you not see
that all of life is at the mercy of God?
He knew he was dying
And he knew he was dying.

I don't know why his nails, his cross
gave him eyes to see
not just a vision of human justice
but a picture of God's unending mercy.
Otherwise, he wouldn't have made
his dying request, would he
sinner that he knew he was —
"Jesus, remember me when you come
into your kingdom"
He wouldn't ask to be remembered
unless he'd heard something Jesus said
— maybe the parable of The Two Sons.

The conversation among three who are dying
gets smaller, now
closer, more intense
it's really just the two of them —
with the whole world overhearing

It's lucky for us they're side by side
and have to speak out
instead of face to face
as they'd like to be,
for our ears are strained already
with trying not to listen.

"Truly, I say to you, today you will be
with me in paradise."

That's (almost) all he says
from the cross.
It must have been something
he really wanted to say.
He knew he was dying
so he promised communion
to his companion in suffering and death.
This is what he gives as King.

The crowd swirled below, yet
some must have had ears to hear
that semi-private speech.
I don't think you'd remember it unless
you knew you were dying.

Jesus of Nazareth, King of the Sinners
— that's what they should have put on that sign
or, King of the Dying
it amounts to the same thing.

It's just as well they didn't, though,
because once the dying see he's King
everything changes, everything lives
He becomes the Lord of Life
and those who know they're dying
know they live

But keep the vision of dying King,
the cross the place of mercy,
and his promise, dying, that he gave the sinner
Today, you will be with me in Paradise
Today, this moment, he is with us
dying as we are
Remember this and live.

Amen.

The Reverend E. Claiborne Jones

In some ways it isn't surprising that I ended up being a preacher. There is a photograph of me, age five, dressed in kilt and best sweater, conducting my entire kindergarten class in some long forgotten song. To be the leader was thrilling. During high school, where chapel was held twice a day and Juniors and Seniors were required to preside, I signed up for extra stints. The "messages" were not particularly profound. Once another student and I read hymns and prayers antiphonally (interesting for me, and the faculty loved it; a bore for all the kids). Another time I eulogized Walt Disney and showed photographs of Mickey and other friends printed in *Paris Match*. I was a ham, at least.

I don't know that these experiences and tendencies shaped my desire to be priest or preacher, though. I had no such desire. The thought of a woman doing such would probably have appalled me. At age sixteen, I had visited Geneva for a week and had determined to be an international lawyer and live in Switzerland forever. My area of expertise would be litigation, however, so that I could stand up in court and make empassioned pleas before a judge and jury.

What I hadn't anticipated as a younger person were the difficulties I would have making sense of a life which, during college, seemed more like a nightmare than the fairytale-come-true I had expected. In school at the University of North Carolina at Chapel Hill, in the town in which I'd grown up, I gradually returned to the parish I had boycotted for several years. I taught Sunday School and helped with this and that, but mainly spent time with the assistant, Bill Coolidge, depending upon him for friendship and acceptance, knowing that he had his own griefs and was willing to listen to mine without desperately putting bandaids on them. I don't recall that we ever talked theology; but it was good, on Sunday morning, that the preacher was a friend, a person whose life was like mine.

This had been true in my childhood as well. David Yates was a great family friend. He always brought ice cream when he came to visit. He sang silly songs and always fell alseep in his chair. When I became ten or so, he taught me how to dance. I stood on his large shoes and we waltzed around the den. And so, when Mr. Yates preached, I sometimes paid attention. At age twelve, after the safety of confirmation, I refused to say the creed (virgin birth? ha!) and Mr. Yates consoled my mother, by saying, "Annie, at least she's paying attention."

And so my vocation as a priest and preacher is grounded in the facts of my history: clergy and preachers were friends, very human; it was fun to be in front of people, talking to them, engendering some attention. And in college, in the middle of my last year, I changed my major to religion, and took ethics and sociology and psychology of religion (everything but Bible) and discovered, nonetheless, that Jesus did not come to teach me how to behave like a good little girl, but rather to love me and all creation and to share and accept our griefs and our joys.

My "professional development" as a preacher was not without its trying moments. Doing Clinical Pastoral Education in a nursing home after one year of seminary and no preaching courses, I crafted a worship service and sermon for the Fourth of July. After the service, I asked one woman in a wheel chair if I could take her back to her room. "No, I'm waiting for the service to begin," she replied. My first "real" sermon, given while a seminary intern in a large downtown parish on the Sunday after Thanksgiving, prompted the rector to say, "That was an adequate essay, Claiborne. It wasn't a sermon." During my deacon year, having had some preaching courses and some practice at preaching, a sermon about community racial tension and Three Mile Island (it was that weekend) prompted a parishioner to write in the search committee self-study, "We don't want a woman who thinks she can preach."

Despite these responses and others, I have kept on preaching and I love it. To do exegesis, and get at some truth about a Biblical text is exciting and very liberating. To try to make sense out of my life in relation to a lesson appointed, not chosen, for the day, is always challenging. To try to be honest with myself and about life in general, and still confess that there is grace amidst the half-truths and unfinished business of being human and being Christian, is strenuous business. And to be, in some strange way, ordained to preach good news is humbling and terrifying. I always pray before I preach, "Lord, please use my words to preach your good news."

I never know what the congregation hears. Each person brings a different life and different meaning to the service. I know I am heard, something is heard, and being female is not an impediment, at least not at Holy Innocents', Atlanta. I heard another woman preach in a service only once in my life, four months ago. It was *wonderful* for me to see, hear, listen to her. And, "I really enjoyed the sermon."

I hope that preaching for every preacher is evolutionary. Mine changes with the community, the season, the intention, world affairs, my life. I cannot say where my preaching is going; it depends on so many factors other than me. I no longer read my sermons or use notes. Preaching is particular word; conversation among people, in one time and place. That in it there may be eternal Word, is by God's grace alone.

April 5, 1981
Holy Innocents' Church
Atlanta, Georgia

I don't usually do sermons like this. I'm not sure it's a sermon. It reads more like a Good Friday meditation. And it must be read, unlike most sermons which I talk out with the congregation on the chancel steps, without notes. This one is too dependent on particular words and phrases to be done without a manuscript. I can't imagine why I made a meditation and told no personal stories except that it was the end of Lent and I was puzzled about the selection of the Lazarus story, a resurrection account, for Lent V, and because I ended up making the sermon, in part, a preface to Holy Week. Also (and this I say after the fact), this is one of my very favorite gospel passages and it speaks to me without my needing to add a story of my own for illumination. In a sense, all I did was to tell the gospel again. And again.

It seems at first glance to be such a simple story . . . A man is taken ill and quickly dies. His sisters, Mary and Martha, grieve deeply for him. Friends come from the city to join them in their grief. Finally, Jesus arrives and they say to him, "If you had been here our brother would not have died." (They must have known he could heal the sick.) Jesus, deeply moved, weeps with them. And then he brings their dead brother back to life. He raises his voice in a great cry, "Lazarus, come forth." And the dead man comes out of the tomb.

It is a very lovely thing which Jesus does — to bring the dead, beloved brother back to life. It seems right that he should do it . . . this Jesus who promises resurrection and life.

But, who among us is not a little envious of Mary and Martha? Who among us has not wished for a death to be undone, deaths which were untimely or senseless or unfair . . . or just too great a loss to bear? Who among us has not wished that a beloved of ours be brought back to life? But it does not happen for us . . . at least, not as it happened for Lazarus and Mary and Martha.

But we are like them, those sisters, in some ways . . . for, knowing the finality of death, knowing the terror of being utterly separated from those we care to love . . . when they also die, who among us has not asked, at one time or another . . . silently, perhaps, "Where were you, God? If you had been here, this pain, this loss, this death would not have happened. Our brother would not have died."

Perhaps the story is not as simple as at first it seemed. For Jesus knew in advance that Lazarus was ill. Mary and Martha had sent for him to come, but

Jesus, *knowing* the man was gravely ill, delayed and did not go to heal his disciples' brother. He did not meet Mary and Martha's expectations at all. And when he arrived, he raised to life a man dead four days and that did not meet Mary and Martha's expectations, either. Jesus' actions seemed nonsensical . . . why did he not come earlier and heal Lazarus? And why did he choose to raise to life Mary and Martha's beloved, while ours remain in the grave?

Is this Jesus someone who is truly for us? Is this Jesus someone we can trust with our lives, with our deaths?

He came to Bethany knowing, surely, that Lazarus had died. He came knowing, no doubt, the anger and disappointment and outrage the sisters must have felt toward him for not coming sooner to help and to heal . . . for not coming at all until four days after the death. He came and heard their blaming of him . . . "If you had been here, our brother would not have died," heard even the whispered words of strangers: "Could not this man, who opened the blind man's eyes, have done something to keep Lazarus from dying?"

And instead of backing off shamefaced, instead of letting them push him away, instead of confirming their suspicion that he just didn't care . . . he was, instead, deeply moved and joined them at the heart of their grief and Jesus wept with them.

And if there was sin there in Bethany, it was in Mary and Martha's believing that Jesus should be at their beck and call, to do their bidding, heal their brother . . . the sin was in Mary and Martha's disappointment, shaming Jesus, pushing him away for not doing what they wanted.

And if there was grace in Bethany, it was Jesus, willing to face all the accusations, to accept the disappointments and outrage; and the grace was Jesus sharing his own grief with them, rejoining them by weeping, honoring them with his tears — these two women whom he so greatly loved.

And so it is with us, I think, and the story is simple after all. There are a thousand ways to try to push God away from us . . . ways to put God to the test and then, if God fails our test, to be done with the whole business. Perhaps the best test is Mary and Martha's . . . to say that God/Jesus doesn't care whether Lazarus lives or dies . . . see he died . . . that proves it . . . to say then that Jesus must not care whether *we* live or die either.

But then, you see, he comes to us and weeps with us and will not let us push him away.

And he commands "come forth" to Lazarus, as if to tell us, "even in the grave, you *cannot* push me away . . . my love will beckon to you even there."

It is a simple story and perhaps explains some of what we do here next week, when, like Mary and Martha, we have high hopes and expectations of Jesus, call him King, wave palms in his pathway, and end up saying only "Crucify him, crucify him. Even that . . . our death sentencing and Jesus' own death . . . cannot push the love of God away . . . for He will say, "Forgive them for they know not what they do." And so it is, with me. Forgive us. Amen.

This is a very recent sermon and is most like what I usually do in terms of both syle and content. I tell stories, I talk about the gospel (parish custom dictates that we preach on the gospel) and it's all done extemporaneously at the top of the sanctuary steps in a modern, fan-shaped, large-yet-intimate eucharistic room. Preaching at Holy Innocents' does seem like an oddly personal conversation with four hundred folks.

Three unusual circumstances surrounded this sermon. I had been on sabbatical for three months and this was the first Sunday back on duty; my mother had had diagnosis of and surgery for colon and liver cancer within the last month; a parish search committee was visiting to hear me preach. As I thought about preparing for the sermon, I realized I must keep to two cardinal rules — say what I needed to say for myself, and speak to the people I know and love at Holy Innocents'. These rules are based on my belief that in the very ordinariness of my life, God works, just as God works in the lives of each of us. Therefore, personal experience and story are how we best know and can communicate that God is with us. Incidentally, I didn't receive a call from the visiting committee. As I was giving the sermon, it occurred to me that they were, in part, listening in on a love letter which was not addressed to them.

I want you to know how glad I am to be here with you. I have been away from Atlanta and from Holy Innocents' for most of the summer – hiking in Montana, studying and playing in California, helping out at Camp Mikell, and visiting my parents in Chapel Hill. It's good to be back. But I must admit that I had a little trepidation about getting back on board at Holy Innocents' after so long an absence. My image of this place is that it's like the moving sidewalk at the airport; and I've thought that coming back would be like a woman I saw this summer who was walking as fast as she could, but still couldn't catch up with the people on the moving sidewalk.

This anxiety about getting back on board became a much greater concern when we found out in early August that my mother had cancer. She was operated on during the week of Faculty pre-service; and I returned to Atlanta at 11:00 Labor Day night, knowing that at 8:00 the next morning, 789 children and 80 or so faculty and staff would be here for the first day of school – my first day back at work.

Well, let me tell you that Holy Innocents' was like a moving sidewalk that morning and I was like the woman walking as fast as she could, trying to catch it.

But what happened is that everyone on this moving sidewalk stretched out both arms to me and pulled me safely aboard, and I thank you. It is good to be here, to be back, to be with you, and to know how much affection there is with us.

Perhaps it is because of my deep appreciation for my relationships with you, then, that I tend to see this morning's gospel also in terms of relationships and the effects of forgiveness on relationships.

A long time ago, I heard a definition of forgiveness I've never forgotten. I don't remember who told me or when. But they said, "At its root, to forgive is to give future to a relationship . . . to give a relationship a chance to change, to grow, to be alive, whether it be between persons, neighborhoods, schools, or countries."

In the gospel this morning, we can see that this is true. The king forgives a debtor 10,000 talents, an inconceivably large sum which can never be repaid (though the servant pretends it can be, with time); and the king restores that man, who was condemned with his family to be enslaved . . . he restores him to freedom. The debtor, whose relationship to his family, home, profession, and past were to be utterly cut off, and whose future was to be virtually severed, is, unbelievably, forgiven. Given a future as a free person, to live again, to function, perhaps even to flourish. This forgiveness is a marvelous, incomparable gift.

One hopes, I think, that, receiving such forgiveness, being restored in his relationships, given a second chance, the debtor will be transformed and extend forgiveness to others as well. But no. When he runs into a fellow who owes him a pittance, an amount easily repaid with time, the debtor condemns him, severs the fellow servant from his family, home, profession, past, and future.

In the end, of course, the unmerciful servant is himself condemned again, and permanently this time. His colleagues, appalled at the way he treats a peer, report him to the king. And the king sentences him, all alone this time, without family, with no hope for freedom, ever. He who would not give future to a relationship with his fellow servant, ends up finally condemning himself to utterly solitary imprisonment for every remaining moment of his own life.

I have chewed on this parable for years and have thought at times that I understood it, had it in the bag. But, as the gospel is wont to do sometimes, this parable has now begun to chew on me. For you see, I am that unmerciful servant . . . I do not find that giving or accepting forgiveness is easy.

When I was five years old, in Mrs. Wettach's kindergarten, which met behind the Porthole restaurant in Chapel Hill, Sandy McMahon socked me in the stomach and knocked the breath out of me. We were playing in the sandbox at the time. I, of course, do not remember anything that I, sweet, demure, innocent little girl that I was, could possibly have done to provoke Sandy McMahon; but I remember what he did to me. Six years later, when I was eleven, all of the "nice" boys and girls in Chapel Hill took social dancing from Mrs. English Bagby and she arranged it so that every girl had to dance with every boy every Friday night. I winced when I had to dance with Sandy McMahon. I tell you all of this because, when I wanted to think of a story to tell you this morning about a time when I found it hard to forgive someone, I thought of Sandy McMahon. Ladies and gentlemen, I am 34 years old, it has been 29 years since Sandy McMahon knocked the breath out of me, and I haven't forgiven him yet.

Another story. Eleven years ago, my sister's first child, three weeks past due, died stillborn because of an incompetent physician. I had just moved to Atlanta a few months before but I got a ride to Myrtle Beach to see Polly for a day. I was a basket case. We all were. That night, I flew back to Atlanta, having made arrangements during the day for my very closest friend in Atlanta to meet me. He was the only person here who knew Polly and my parents and was a treasured college buddy. Well, I got to the airport late that night, and he wasn't there. He had called someone else to meet me.

I had a hard time remembering this story, not because it is less painful than having the breath knocked out of me, but because I forgave my college friend so many many years ago. And it wasn't easier to forgive him than Sandy McMahon because it hurt less to be stood up at the airport that sad night than to be punched in the stomach . . . it hurt much more . . . But it was easier to forgive because I wanted so much for that friendship to live, to grow. And today, he and his wife and his children are my close and dearest friends. The last thing I wanted with Sandy McMahon was for our relationship to grow and it didn't. It died in that sandbox.

Now I am confident that in God's economy it is as important for me to forgive Sandy as to forgive my close friend. With my luck, Sandy's probably a bishop somewhere and I'll end up in his diocese. And perhaps now that I've so thoroughly confessed all of this to you, I can forgive him at last. But then again, perhaps I am a bit too much like that unmerciful servant.

And now to the other side of the coin. Like the unmerciful servant, it is hard for me to accept forgiveness, to really receive it. Undoubtedly, the person who has forgiven me the most so far in my life is my mother. I was not a nice, sweet, kid. I was a crumb. I suppose the most tangible wrongs I did her were to carve Watts Poe's name in the top of an eighteenth-century desk and to draw on silk lampshades, but there were many, many more wrongs, much more severe . . . constant bickering, petty criticisms designed to hurt, taking pleasure in shocking or shaming her, and, perhaps above all others, a patronizing, cold and hostile analysis of why she was an "inadequate mother." All the while, she forgave, accepted, and loved me, amidst her hurt and her confusion and her disappointment. I would ignore it all, or pretend to. I acted, often, as if I didn't want or need her forgiveness or acceptance or concern. I could do it on my own, thank you very much, no help from you. A bit like an unmerciful servant I know.

Mother was undeterred and all along forgave and forgave and forgave so that when, finally, by God's grace I began to recognize and accept and be grateful for her forgiveness of me, it hadn't diminished a bit. Her unflagging forgiveness has made it possible, even now, for our relationship to live, to have a future, to change, to flourish, to grow. All it needed was my willingness to accept her forgiveness, to receive it gladly. And now we have a future, for however long, together.

A most amazing thing happened last week. My mother called me at the office to chat. Friends, this is not done in the Jones family. I doubt if my mother called my father at his office more than five times in forty-four years. But my mother called me at 2:05 on a Tuesday afternoon to chat. It was wonderful. We laughed and smiled and I asked how her recovery from surgery was going and she said, "Claiborne, there's only one thing I want you to know. I've given very specific instructions to the doctors that whoever tries to get me into a hospital again is to be murdered on the spot, D.O.A." And we laughed again. But there was a meaning here, for she and I know that I am the one who finally, after two years of illness, got her to go to the doctor to find out what was the matter, in late July. And then she said to me, "Claiborne, I love you." And, in the Jones family, that isn't done either. And it seems a miracle to me, that a relationship can have such life to it, such surprise, such a future, if only forgiveness is given and received.

There is a story about a fellow, middle-aged, disgruntled in adolescence with the church, whose life finally brings him to the point of wanting to go to church again. So he church hops Sunday after Sunday, dissatisfied, until he happens into an Episcopal Church during the middle of the service and hears a congregation on its knees saying, "We have done those things which we ought not to have done and we have left undone those things which we ought to have done . . ." and he smiled and said, "Sounds like my kind of crowd." Isn't that wonderful? For it is our crowd, you and me, of whom he speaks. We who believe in God's forgiveness, we who no longer need to hide our fears or our mistakes from each other, who no longer need to live in prideful isolation as if we didn't need each other, for we are forgiven people, again and again. Christ is not like the king who forgives once and then condemns. At last count, among us, Christ had forgiven seven million times seventy trillion times. And it happens not only as we kneel together in this place. It can happen even as we remember sandboxes from long ago, even as we are *not* greeted by friends in airports, even as we learn to say good-bye before it's too late in words like, "I love you." Amen.

SERMON TO THE SENIORS
Matthew 19:16-26

June 2, 1984
St. Margaret's School
Tappahannock, Virginia

I graduated from St. Margaret's School in Tappahannock, Virginia, in 1968. In a sense, I had grown up there. My oldest sister enrolled in 1960 when I was ten. I loved St. Mag's and still treasure friendships from those days. I was and am especially fond of Viola Woolfolk, who was Headmistress throughout the years my family sent kids to SMS. Miss Woolfolk's last year was 1983-84, and she asked me to give the Sermon to the Seniors that June. I wanted to do something which would convey what I had learned at St. Margaret's, and to make enough connections with the students listening so that I might bridge the generation gap a bit. I had to select a lesson and picked the rich young man because he represents what we so often aspire to as young adults and older adults. The story from my own experience at SMS is not the same as the one I originally intended to use. I talked the sermon out to a friend late Friday, the night before the trip to Virginia, and he said the story I originally chose (about another student cheating and my self-righteousness) was too hard on me and, after all, was saying too much about another's wrong doing, as well. Later still, I cried some, unexpectedly, and realized again how important it was for me to do well for the teachers and Head and school who had given so much to me. The sermon went well. There was a lot of laughter. And, in a sense, I saw the place more clearly than ever before, and said good-bye again.

This is a happy occasion and a happy time for me. When Miss Woolfolk asked me in October to give the baccalaureate, I was thrilled that I would have a good excuse to come back to St. Margaret's for this wonderful weekend. I'm glad to be here. Let me say, however, that as June got closer and closer, my enthusiasm and excitement were more and more overshadowed by anxiety. You see, to many of you I am a grown-up coming back to preach; but the last time I was in the room, I was a high school senior and my teachers are still here, sitting in the back of the chapel. In 1968, neither they nor I expected I would be back at St. Margaret's wearing long robes and preaching to them! The other point of anxiety about being here today is that, as the younger sister of two SMS alums, and a student here myself, I have heard eight sermons to the seniors and eight graduation addresses and, frankly, I do not remember them as the highlight of the weekend. The miracle is that out of those sixteen, I actually remember one address, my senior year. The speaker talked about "if onlys" and said for us not to go through life saying "If only I had made such and such a choice" or "If only I hadn't done so and so." Instead, he encouraged us to live life fully, without regret . . . to live for today and tomorrow and not feel bound by our past mistakes. I remember being taught here that what we celebrate tomorrow is a commencement, not a graduation, a new beginning for all of you here in the front rows.

I think the reason I remember that graduation address is that I am an "if only" person. If only I had studied harder in Mrs. Sanborn's World Problems class during the tax section, then perhaps I wouldn't have been audited by the Georgia authorities last year. If only I had not brought my St. Margaret's yearbook to the school where I am chaplain, perhaps the students there would never have known that my nickname here was "Claibby Baby." If only I hadn't eaten so many of those wonderful homemade rolls, perhaps I would have met the man of my dreams at a Christ Church social and my whole life would be different. In the larger scope of my life, these are really rather small regrets. And my life will always have its share of them. I think the graduation speaker in 1968 was speaking more in terms of major choices and major regrets, which brings me to the story we heard in the lesson tonight. A peculiar story about a young man who wants to know how he can be assured of eternal life. It's rather strange that this should be a concern of his. My seventh-grade Bible students read the story recently and one of them said, "He must not have been very happy if he was worried about eternal life when he's young and rich." If any of you showed great concern about eternal life at your age, your parents and teachers would be quite concerned for you. But, nonetheless, we have this young man asking Jesus how he can receive eternal life and Jesus simply replies, "You know the answer, follow the commandments." Well, the young man apparently has done that, but he's still not satisfied. Apparently, goodness isn't enough for him and so, the text says, Jesus' heart warmed to him, and he looked at him and said, "Sell all you have, give to the poor and come, follow me." And the young man's face falls and he goes away with a heavy heart for he has great wealth.

I wonder about the young man's "if only." Perhaps he thought, "If only Jesus hadn't asked me to do that" or, perhaps, later in life, "If only I had chosen to do as Christ asked."

It is puzzling. We have here a person who is good and wealthy, moral and successful, and it is not enough. Strange — for success, accomplishing your goals, and morality, living a life that is good for you and your neighbors, are most of what your parents and teachers and St. Margaret's school have tried to teach you all these years, no? But he leaves Jesus with a heavy heart, wealthy and good and alone. You see, Jesus said, "Sell all you have and give to the poor and *come*, follow me." What seems at first a demand to live in poverty is really an invitation to friendship. Jesus says to the young fellow "Come and be my buddy," but he knows that this young man will not be free to accept that invitation, will not be able to accept that loving look, as long as he is a prisoner of wealth.

When I was at St. Margaret's I was both good and successful. I had been president of my class both my sophomore and junior years, was on honor council and on honor roll. And I knew, to the core of my being, that I would be elected president of the student body. It was obvious. We had a school meeting in the chapel and the floor was opened for nominations. One person was nominated, and then another. Finally, Bakel Wirsing, who was in eighth grade, nominated me. I was the fifth and the last. At first I was a little concerned, but figured that it was just so obvious to everyone that I would be elected that no one remembered to nominate me.

Later in the day my best friend, Jan Kinzer, who was the current president of the student body, found me and asked me to withdraw my name from the race. I couldn't believe it, and asked her why in the world I should do such a thing. And she looked at me with love and said, "Claiborne, you have been an expletive deleted all year long and you haven't a prayer of winning, but if you withdraw it will give somebody decent a chance to win." Well, I was shocked. I wouldn't believe what she was saying, but I knew it was true. I was good and self-righteous. I was successful and arrogant and in my conceit I was all alone. Thanks to Jan Kinzer, and her loving courage, my senior year at St. Margaret's was one of the happiest in my life. I set aside some of the arrogance and conceit, made a little room for people to love me, and opened a little window to love some other people. It was a deliberate, conscious choice to put friendship ahead of success and goodness.

I am now chaplain at an Episcopal school. We have 785 students from age three to eighth grade and it is not where I ever thought I'd end up when I graduated from St. Margaret's. The children in the school call me Chaplain Claiborne, but a few years ago, the 4-year-olds misunderstood and thought my name was Chocolate Clayferd. And the next year the 4's thought it was Chaplain Playground. Isn't it wonderful? To be called Chocolate and Playground by 4-year-olds is the highest of praise. More importantly, it occurs to me that they love me. I am neither as wealthy nor as good as I thought I would be by now, when I graduated 16 years ago; but I am richer than I ever imagined I could possibly be, because of the people who love me.

I read a story recently about a little girl and her mother who visited a sculptor's studio each day, watching the artist carve a lion out of a huge block of marble. Finally, one day, the animal's figure was clear, and the child recognized what it was. She turned to her mother and said, "Mom, how did that man know that there was a lion in there?" As we, all of us, of any age continue to grow and to flourish, I hope we will remember that it is, finally, love alone which sets us free, Christ's love, offered to us through 4-year-olds, and grandparents, teachers, and friends who have the courage to tell the truth. Christ's love alone sets us free to be ourselves, whether we are wealthy or poor, famous or unknown, good or not so good. In my yearbook my senior year, a friend wrote, "Claibby, remember how many of us love you just for being you." Remember how many people love you, just for being you.

The Reverend Camille S. Littleton

My church background, at the Church of St. Michael and All Angels, Anniston, Alabama, is a strong one. The people there, priest, organist-choirmaster, Sunday School teachers, friends, all shaped in a very positive way my understanding of God and God's love for me and others.

I was a member of the choir, participated in youth group activities, and felt the church to be my home and the people my family. We must have had very good liturgy and I received good training; I know we had good music. My strong interest in liturgy and music stay with me and are strengths I bring to worship and my ministry today.

As many people do, I gave up most of my church involvement when I was in college (Auburn University) and during my early twenties. It was my time of rebellion, but also a dark time of discontent. When I did start back to church it was mostly because of my 18-month-old daughter; I wanted her to experience the church in a way similar to the way I remembered it.

In 1970 I moved to Atlanta. When I did start back to church the prayer book was in the process of revision. It was like a breath of fresh air to hear the church express what I had been feeling, that God can be worshipped in many ways, that new words and images help express our understanding of God and give us fresh insights into God's love. I entered church life full force, teaching Sunday School, cooking meals, attending classes, asking questions, reading, studying, hungry to know. In the searching I began to feel again a spark.

It seemed to me the church all along had challenged and encouraged me to use all my talents and to develop my abilities. Yet, when I felt called to do so through ordination, the church, some of it at least, was indignant, even seemed to have been betrayed. For the church to say that females could not be ordained seemed contrary to all I had been taught.

Not all people were indignant, however, and many encouraged me and others to seek ordination. I found myself invited to speak to many groups who were interested, suspicious, curious, even hostile about what I was doing; I inspired some, angered others. The time from 1974 until 1976, when ordination passed in General Convention, was a roller coaster for me emotionally. It seemed I did not know how I would be received in any setting I entered. We all struggled through.

My intuitive understandings gleaned from the church as a child and formed as I grew in the early 70s needed a language. Seminary at Candler School of Theology, speaking to groups, and listening to people and ideas began to give me the words and added new dimensions to my theology and life as we find it. Much of my sermon preparation involves looking for words, concepts, and images to articulate connections between what I sense in the scripture and in the life of the parish at a particular time.

As a deacon and a priest, I have been at two churches, one small suburban church and one large inner-city church. People at both places have responded to me in similar ways, mostly very positively. I don't know what fundamental differences there are in male and female clergy (or parishioners). All of us have our own sets of gifts and abilities; all of us are shaped in individual and corporate ways; all of us are products of a fallen world. What I do know is that there needs to be a balance, that men and women have to work together for mutual joy and reconciliation, peace and harmony, and to care for children and the world.

Women in the pulpit and at the altar have enriched the church and the lives of parishioners. For centuries only one-half of humanity has stood in those places and we have had only a half-life experience. The struggles, the prejudices are not gone; but I see some changes.

I have been at St. James', Marietta, for almost five years. Children there take for granted that women are priests, that God is both male and female, although they probably would not express it that way yet. My daughter is almost 16. She and her friends take for granted some of the equality and the status of women gained in the world and the church, and assume they will do whatever they want to do when they grow up. For that I am grateful; perhaps they can spend their energy righting other wrongs in the world.

EPIPHANY VIII
Isaiah 49:8-18
I Corinthians 4:1-13
Matthew 6:24-34

February 26, 1984
St. James' Church
Marietta, Georgia

So often scripture passages speak to us where we are, even lectionary texts published and prescribed years ago to be read years later. That was so much the case for this sermon. My mother had been ill for several months; her death came sooner than we expected. I felt very vulnerable but listened to two friends who encouraged me to preach about the experience. I am grateful to them. It is still a profound part of my own story; how fitting for me that it was the season of Epiphany, when God is seen.

I am grateful also that I have carried and given birth to a child. Before women could be ordained, no congregation could hear its priest talk about that particular experience. I feel gratified to give that to St. James'. Being a daughter and a mother shaped this sermon for me.

There are two threads which I have woven together from today's lessons. From the Gospel of Matthew, Jesus is teaching about life. He says, "Do not be anxious about your life. Is not life more than food, and the body more than clothing?" And He goes on in what is a familiar passage to most of us. He talks about the lilies of the field and the birds. The birds have all they need, the lilies of the field have splendid colors. And God takes care of all that, he tells them. Therefore certainly human beings will have all that they need.

This type of speaking that Jesus is doing has been called "wisdom sayings." When it is written down it's called "wisdom literature." That is, teachings or sayings that can be found in the Bible, in other cultures, in our life today which help us lead a happy life, which add order and peace. When the wise of every culture pass on what they have learned, it's called wisdom teachings or wisdom literature. So Jesus says, "Do not be anxious," because that is a way of adding order and peace to our lives.

Jesus in His wisdom is saying that there are things that we cannot control, but that we are taken care of, and therefore we are not to worry.

We all know that at some level and we all know that things will be given to us in this life which we will not understand. It helps to be reminded that undergirding all of us and undergirding this universe, we proclaim a force and a power which is mighty and which is everpresent.

There are those who would have us think that Jesus was not concerned with life, only with conquering death, or life after death. We can point to passages in the scriptures, however, that indicate that Jesus was very much concerned with the present, with the here and now. He wanted very much to teach his disciples then and his disciples today how best to function in the world. If the only meaning in life were to come to us after death, why would there be so much emphasis on the present life here? And why would he have taught that we are to feed the sheep and to care for the people and to heal the sick and to go and spread the Good News?

There is no doubt in my mind that I'm an anxious person. I suspect that most of you have your anxieties too. Some of my anxieties I can laugh at. Others are everpresent with me. I worry about paying bills, about how children are growing up in the world, my own child. I worry about how I will be received and perceived by other people. I worry if I make a wrong bid at bridge. I worry if I keep someone behind me who's honking the horn even though I'm not ready to turn. I worry about things like that and I'm anxious. Some of those are silly and I can laugh at them, and some of them are everpresent with me.

However, I have noticed that in critical times of my life something other than anxiety has taken over and has helped me through. Perhaps so I could be anxious again. But that's another story.

The second thread is from Paul. He says we are called to be stewards of the mysteries of God. Mystery is a word which we use to explain what we can't explain. We more or less agree that somehow God has something to do with mystery. But when we don't have any more words to describe what we're trying to say, we say, "It's a mystery." That's very valid. Sometimes that is the most faithful response we can make, because it affirms a power and presence greater than ourselves.

My life has been touched deeply during the past two weeks. Many of you know of the death of my mother. Many of you have responded to me with caring during that time. You've cared for me here and now in the face of the mystery of death.

Two weeks ago on a Monday I decided on the spur of the moment to go to my hometown. I had already changed my day off and planned to go on Tuesday. But that evening I just decided to go and to take my daughter out of school. We arrived there Monday evening and we went to the hospital. We saw my mother. She was in more pain and on more medication than I had ever seen her before. Later that night we were called back to the hospital. She had died just minutes before my father and I arrived.

We sat there together in the room not saying very much, occasionally speaking to each other, mainly just being silent together. Eventually I walked over to the bed where she lay and I touched her hand. At that moment something very strange occurred to me. Death has always seemed such a mystery to me, something that I could not fathom; but in that moment something else happened. At that moment I remembered almost fifteen years ago when I had the same mysterious feelings holding my newborn daughter in my arms. I was amazed. I was in awe. I thought then as I thought two weeks ago, this is a *mystery*. I don't understand this. Holding my newborn daughter in my arms, watching her very tentative movements and feeling amazed and awed by this little life in my hands; standing there holding my dead mother's hand and watching the stillness, that too was amazing and I was awed.

Surely the two mysteries of life are birth and death. These events we can never understand fully. I don't think we will ever know what it is that happens at the moment of life or at the moment of death. Neither all of our science nor all of our speculation will ever tell us that, because that is in God's realm.

What we can do is to tell the story of our birth, of our life, and of the lives and deaths of those we love, what they mean to us and what they meant to us, how they touched us and how they shaped us. It is in telling the story and telling our story, that we begin to share with each other. We begin to see we all have anxieties, that we all have strengths and weaknesses and loneliness. But along with that is amazement and wonder and mystery, if we let ourselves experience it.

Something that is amazing is something that does not connect with other experiences we have had in life. When we share our stories we begin to see that somehow we are connected to others, even though in that one moment of the mystery we stand alone with God. In that moment to be alone with God in the mystery of it all is good.

Someone wrote that all we need to do is take a first step when we can't see what the next steps will be. Being anxious people, we want to know exactly what the next steps will be. But we need to know and understand that we can never fully understand. But we can also understand that people have gone before us and people will come after us who live in these same mysteries of God.

Being a good steward of these mysteries must have something to do with having respect and reverence for the most profound moments of life.

LENT IV
I Samuel 6:1-13
Ephesians 5:1-14
John 9:1-38

April 1, 1984
St. James' Church
Marietta, Georgia

In preparing for any sermon, I begin to look for patterns throughout the lectionary texts or within one of the texts. I find it to be interesting, almost like seeking pieces of a jigsaw puzzle that will fit together. The "pattern" in this gospel was the questions, and I was reminded of the questions we ask each other, and God.

We all know there are so many questions and so few answers. Our confession is that we will know, someday. Our response, then, seems to me to be to discern which questions can be answered.

You can probably see shades of previous sermons in this one. I find many of my sermons speak to an undergirding unity which at its core is a mystery.

The gospel today is filled with questions. It begins with questions by the disciples: "Rabbi, who sinned, this man or his parents, that he was born blind?" Once the man was healed, more questions from the Pharisees: "How did he do this?" From the neighbors: "Who is this man?" Again from the Pharisees to the parents: "Is this your son?" And again, "How did he do this?" Finally, a question from Jesus: "Do you believe in the son of man?"

A lot of questions, rather like the questions we ask of ourselves and others. We ask: "Why was one born blind? Why is one child born deformed and another whole? Why is one person murdered and another not? Why does one person recover from a disease? Why does another die from the same disease? Why does one die suddenly and why does another have to suffer and linger on sometimes seemingly forever, in pain?"

Children ask a lot of questions, don't they? "Why is rain wet?" "Why is grass green?" Probably you asked your parents questions like that, or you have tried to answer questions like that from your children. We try to answer questions, and we do a pretty good job sometimes. For instance, we know from science that there is a substance which scientists have labeled chlorophyll and that chlorophyll is in grass; it gives grass its green color. We can tell our children that grass is green because it has chlorophyll in it. And then, they ask, "Why?" So we struggle and say that chlorophyll acts with light from the sun and "does something" to make plants green . . . and hope that satisfies them.

To the question of rain that is wet, we say that rain is water and water is wet. They ask, "Why?" and we say that oxygen and hydrogen come together and make water. But if they keep pushing us with that "why" question, we will have to say something eventually that is unscientific: "I don't know," "Go ask your dad," "God made it that way."

I noticed something in this story from the gospel. Jesus did not try to answer the questions about why the man was born blind or who had sinned. The Pharisees came from a tradition that said if someone had an illness or a disease, it was because he or she had sinned and the sin was showing up in the person's body. So for them, it may have been an honest kind of searching. For Jesus, however, that was not the question. The question was how God will be glorified in this situation.

God has never told us why; we do not know why things happen the way they do. If you think back over your knowledge of the scriptures, you will notice that we are seldom told "why" things happen other than for God's glory. We are given responses to the way the world is: God's response to the world, our response to the world, to God, to other people.

We know some of the responses. God's response to us is a steadfast, loving covenant to God's creation. Our response is to a loving creator. Some of what we must do is commanded in scriptures. We must love our neighbor; we must love God; we must feed the hungry; we must be healers and reconcilers; we must seek forgiveness and be forgiving. We must be merciful and compassionate and caring people. Why? Because God would have it that way.

The Hebrews for centuries attributed all of these qualities to God; and when we find ourselves fitting our lives into what God expects and what God desires, we find we are living the abundant life. We find when we feed people, we are enriched as they are; we find when we go and sit in the hospital with someone who is sick, we and they become enriched. We find when we sit silently and meditate or listen for God's word to us, we are enriched. "Why?" Because God has set up creation that way.

The issue is the same for us as it was for Jesus in the story. How will God be glorified in a situation? How will God be glorified in the situations of our life? Should we meet a hungry person, should we meet a lonely person, should we see a child being abused, should we see injustice anywhere, "How will God be glorified by my presence in this situation?" is our question.

Our question, then, is not "why" something is the way it is. Perhaps we need not torture ourselves, or spin our wheels with that question. Perhaps the only question for us is, "In light of what I see in the world, in any given situation, how may I serve, Lord? How may I glorify you, God? What is my response to you and to others in need?" Amen.

PENTECOST VI
Amos 7:7-15
Ephesians 1:1-14
Mark 6:7-13

July 11, 1982
St. James' Church
Marietta, Georgia

I was reading a lay person's introduction to physics as I began preparing for this sermon. It hit me in a new way that Amos was speaking about a physical law (later named gravity by Newton) to describe God's response to Israel. I began to think more about science and religion.

I bypassed all the physics, chemistry, science, and math courses that I could in college. Now I am eager to know these theories and am even more fascinated to think of putting them into theological terms. Annie Dillard is a favorite author of mine. It is amazing to me that everything, according to physicists, might be atoms; that according to mathemeticians, between two numbers, there is infinity. I feel a kind of humbling silence about the intimate structures of the universe.

Of all things that seem unlikely to me, I have been reading a physics book. It's rather a history of physics, the theories and discoveries of scientists through the centuries. I have found it interesting. My science background is very limited. I don't think of myself as someone who knows or is interested in science, physics, or complicated things like that. Much of this book I don't understand. However, it gives me, as a reader, almost a picture of the structure of the universe. And at times, the author relates scientific findings and theories to what Christian theologians and world religions all over have believed for centuries. The point is that science and religion are very close in their goals. That is, to know what life is like and what life is about, why it is that way. My reading this week took me to a theory which physicists claim, that things have a tendency to flow from order to disorder. The example used is that a drop of ink will expand in a glass of water so that it is no longer a drop of ink, it is no longer contained within itself, but is spread throughout the water. We all know that, but I didn't know it was a scientific theory.

Also this week, I have been moving. I have moved my living place from one place to another. I have gained a sense of satisfaction throwing out the clutter that has acquired over the past two years and some of it over the past ten or twelve years. All of us know about clutter, it's like that drop of ink. It is like one piece of paper that seems to multiply more and more until it could fill a house. It seemed to me this week that the more I threw out the more there was to throw out. I'll admit I'm not a good housekeeper, but I don't know where most of that clutter came from. Then there is the question of dust. No matter how often you dust furniture or books, there is more dust in a very short time. It just *comes* from somewhere.

No matter how hard we struggle to keep order — dust furniture, get rid of clutter, maintain relationships, or even our lives — it seems there is a tendency in this world for disorder to come from order. No matter how much order there is or how much order we think there is, disorder always comes.

Amos discovered that. He's not the first, he's not the last, but he is the one we read about this morning. His life was going the way he thought it was to go. He was a herdsman and a dresser of sycamore trees. He had no inclination to become a prophet, and yet he felt God calling him to be a prophet. In fact, he seems to have had a vision that God had dropped a plumb line from heaven to earth so that Amos could see how the world was crumbling, and that God's vision was straight and that God would maintain that vision for Israel even if Israel would not.

That's another physical theory, the plumb line. My father is a civil engineer and I used to be interested in his tools. One of those was a plumb bob. It was a metal object on a string, about six inches long, very heavy to be so small. He told me that gravity kept that string straight so that he could measure angles and be accurate. Gravity is one of the laws of the universe as we know it. Things stay down and a plumb line gives us a straight line, up and down, so things can be measured accurately.

It has always been interesting to me that God used a plumb line to determine and to show Amos that things were not the way they should be in Israel, and that Amos would be called out from his herds and his trees in order to teach that. The people of Israel didn't want to hear it, and he didn't want to say it. His orderly life was disrupted by a vision of God putting a plumb line and telling Amos that he would be the one to speak about the condition of the world.

Paul also gives us an image this morning, I think, of the way the universe is structured, of the way life is. He uses no scientific terms. Nor does he use a plumb line. He does not talk about order or disorder in those terms but he says very simply, "We are created by the Creator. He intends that we be in relationship with the Creator as children, as children of God." Furthermore, Paul says that God has sent his son, Jesus, in order that when we fail, when the disorders of our lives overwhelm us, and we either fail to act or act in wrong or hurtful ways, we will be redeemed and forgiven.

There is a spirit, which we call the Holy Spirit, which is forever restoring order into the disorder of our lives. Theologians have called this the Trinity. Physicists may have some other word for how creation came to be or whatever process it is that brings order from disorder. Nevertheless, we are talking about being in harmony and living orderly lives in which we can be peaceful, blessed, happy people. Perhaps it means being called out from a comfortable life. Perhaps it means expanding our limits beyond what we know, beyond our very given lives at this moment. Perhaps it means "taking in," compressing rather than expanding. Perhaps the disorder is in various aspects of our lives and we need to pull the reins in and focus our energies on the order.

We are called, each one of us, by God, because we are created by God, because we have been redeemed, forgiven, and blessed by God and because there is a loving, caring spirit which can bring us out of disorder into order. We may be called to stay or to go. Nevertheless, we are called and any time we are called, it is to maintain or to achieve order so that we can be flowing, fluid, harmonious children of God.

Why the world was created in a way that seems to move toward disorder is not our question. We don't know that; perhaps someday we will know that. We don't know why lives are upturned and upset, we don't know why people suffer, why healthy bodies become ill and weakened. We don't know those answers. All we need to know is that at the core of the universe there is a loving Creator, who created us and who calls us to maintain creation, who calls us to seek order, to dust, to tend the garden, to care for children, to care for the lonely, to tend to things that are disorderly and, thereby, be partners in creation. Partners with God, seeking order in the midst of disorder. Amen.

Lori M. Lowe

When people find out what I do, the first question they ask is: "What do you call a woman priest?" — to which I can offer no totally satisfactory answer. The second most often asked question is: "Whatever made you decide to do that?" — which often brings me to reflect on the experiences of my life that have shaped who I am and who I am becoming.

My heritage would seem to set the stage. On my father's side of the family, my grandfather, Samuel F. Lowe, was a Southern Baptist preacher. We went to church regularly, where my father was a deacon and taught a Sunday school class for many years. My sister, Kathy, and I sang in children's choirs and were in numerous Christmas pageants. Mother was in the women's auxiliary and the adult choir. My childhood memories are filled with Bible stories heard in Sunday school, fragments of once memorized Psalms, the sounds of hymns and sacred music, Easter dresses, revivals, and altar calls.

I was especially impressed when from time to time our church was visited by missionaries. They were usually a husband and wife team who would tell of their ministries in faraway places. I was fascinated, and for many years thought I wanted to be a missionary. Those missionary women were my first female role models in the church, and I look back on that now as an early experience of my calling.

But I did not really want to be a missionary, and I was not entirely satisfied in the Southern Baptist tradition. I was pleased when I was in my early teens, my family joined a nearby Methodist church, and I became active in the youth group and choir.

When I was 15 or 16, I visited an Episcopal church for the first time. Although I was lost in the prayer book and the "ups" and "downs" of the service, I was deeply touched by the rich drama of liturgical worship. I began to attend the Episcopal church regularly and learned my way through the liturgy quickly, feeling very much at home in the Catholic tradition. In addition to the appeal of liturgical worship and the sacraments, I was also attracted to the "roominess" of Anglican theology. As soon as I could take the necessary classes, I was confirmed.

Looking back on it now, it seems like a rather radical thing for an adolescent girl to do on her own. Although my father's family was shocked and expressed some criticism, my parents encouraged me to make my own decision. I think that with so many young people dropping out of church altogether, they were glad to see me going to church, even if they may have been a little skeptical about the one I chose.

Perhaps it was a way to establish my independence while still having some important needs met. And I had some pretty big needs. My father was seriously ill for three years before he died. I was 18 years old; I loved him dearly and it was a devastating loss. My faith was crucial to my surviving that blow.

And I did survive. I went to college, married my high school sweetheart, earned my bachelor's degree, and began to teach school. I taught high school English, and I loved it! I loved using literature as a way to talk about life, values, relationships, emotions, and ideas. And I loved the kids and the way I was able to relate to them, listen to them, encourage them. I knew I wanted to do something with all that, and to earn an advanced degree, but I didn't know *what*. Something like teaching, but not exactly; something like counseling, but not exactly. But what? It would be some years before I began to know.

During those years I had my three wonderful children, Melissa, David, and Justin. I had the opportunity to be at home with them for a few years, but I was also involved in church and community activities, and often worked part-time.

One of those part-time jobs was teaching at night in an adult high school program. Teaching again stirred up some of my earlier yearnings for more education, and about future directions. At the same time, I was experiencing new satisfaction in a variety of lay ministries in a small parish and in some of the church's renewal movements of the 1970s. With hindsight, I see that pieces of the puzzle were beginning to fall into place.

Ordination of women to the priesthood was officially approved by the General Convention of the Episcopal Church in 1976; an event I observed with approval but little emotion. But within a year or two, I began to think about "ordained ministry" as a possibility in my own future.

Thinking of it as "ordained ministry" was fine; that meant study and work. Thinking of it as "priesthood" was another matter. That had connotations of identity and authority that scared me to death. I was, after all, a suburban housewife with three children, a ranch-style house, and a station wagon with wood sides. Who was I to think of being a priest? I could hardly imagine it, but the idea persisted and I could not ignore it. I considered the possibility that it was a neurotic symptom, or a call from God, or both. As a way of checking out those possibilities, I enrolled in the Diocese of Atlanta's pre-seminary program, known then as Experiment in Ministry. That year included some invaluable insights into my own personal issues, and a deep desire to continue towards ordination and parish ministry.

In 1981 I entered the Episcopal Studies Program at Candler School of Theology, Emory University. Candler is a large, diverse seminary in an urban setting. From the first day, I was hooked. I tried to experience all of it — the traditional course work, the student activities, the organizations concerned with social justice, the worship, and most of all, my self. I began to experience myself in new ways: as a person with an identity and a vocation, as well as someone with a family and relationships. It was exciting, but not easy, and *everything* was not going well. I was separated and divorced during my middle and senior years of seminary.

People who know that often ask me if my vocational aspirations caused my marriage to end. It's a difficult question to address because the answer is complex, and because I am reluctant to speak publicly about personal things that also involve others. At the risk of gross oversimplification, I can say this: the changes in me and the focus of my activities did, of course, affect my marriage. It was not, I believe, my particular vocation that brought about the crisis, but the stress and change heaped on long-buried problems.

It was, as so many people know these days, an incredibly painful experience. I learned firsthand about brokenness, healing, forgiveness, and grace.

I finished my Master of Divinity degree and graduated in May of 1983. In the fall, I was hired as Pastoral Assistant at St. Bartholomew's, Atlanta. That's a title sometimes used to describe one who is "trained but not ordained." My ministry there is full and rich. With the exception of sacramental functions, I've had the invaluable experience of the whole range of parish ministry.

As the larger Church has struggled with the ordination and deployment of women, and with difficult issues of marriage and divorce (especially among its clergy), I have had a number of delays in the ordination process. At this writing, I am a Postulant for Holy Orders, and the community at St. Bartholomew's has wholeheartedly endorsed me for the next step. I am "in the process" again, moving toward, God willing, the diaconate and the priesthood.

So when someone asks me that question — "Whatever made you decide to do that?!" I sometimes answer a little flippantly with a line like, "God only knows." The answer may take a lifetime of reflection.

February 7, 1984
St. Bartholomew's Church
Atlanta, Georgia

This gospel reading, with its beautiful Christological interpretation of the law, is full of possibilities for the preacher. But what I kept coming back to in my reflections was that last line with its ". . . be perfect . . ."!

One of the things I have struggled with in my life has been the terrible need to be perfect. Having begun to come to terms with the reality of not being perfect — and the gracefulness of not having to be — I could not ignore this seemingly pejorative demand. So I began to ask questions of the text and of this line in particular. How could one be perfect? What is perfect? What does "perfect" mean here? What's the good news, the gospel, in the command to be perfect?

This sermon is the result (at least, at this point in time) of struggling with those questions; of looking for the good news in ". . . be perfect . . . ."

The following layout is a reproduction of the way I write my manuscripts for reference in the pulpit.

"You, therefore, must be perfect, as your heavenly Father is perfect."

There was a popular movie out
  a few years ago —
    with Dudley Moore and Julie Andrews.
    It was a fairly good movie,
    actually — about the
    evolution of a relationship
    during a sort of male menopause crisis.
      What the movie is
        best remembered for,
          however, is the
            title *(10)* and
              Bo Derek.

The meaning of the title was
that Bo Derek was the
PERFECT 10; the most beautiful
woman imaginable; the standard
by which all others were measured;
the BEST.

Lori M. Lowe *Epiphany VII*

Long after the movie left the theaters,
   the phrase — "A TEN" —
      continues to carry those
         connotations:
            The Most Beautiful (or Handsome),
            The Highest Standard
            The Best.

That's not a new concept really.
   Just a phrase, a name,
      an identification of
         something we've
            always known;
      SOMEBODY OUT THERE IS PERFECT.
      . . . and it's not me!

It's something that's particularly
   true of our experience as children.
      I remember when I was
         in elementary school —
            and even high school —
         I *longed* to be "a ten."
         I would have given
            anything to have been
            one of those perfectly
            gorgeous girls with
thick, long hair, perfect figures,
wonderful personalities, *and* brains.
   I had — I was sure —
      the worst hair,
         the most "uneventful" figure,
            the most dull personality,
               and the least "brains"!

The incredible — and sad —
thing about this experience
is that it is almost universal.
Even the people you and I thought
of as "tens," were miserably sure
they were zeros —
   were full of self-doubt,
      and wished to be
         somehow
            PERFECT —
   and knew themselves to
      fall short.

It's a powerful, powerful
   force —
      that longing to be
         Perfect.

Actually, I think it's a longing
   to be loved, and mixed up
      with the notion that to be
         loved, we must be perfect.

"PERFECT" is a word or a concept
that's loaded with all kinds of
meanings for us.

   When we hear in today's gospel,
      "You, therefore, must be perfect . . ."
         (and as if that weren't enough)
      ". . . as your heavenly Father is
   perfect!"
         — when we hear that,
many of us *flinch* —
   as if, once again
      we are faced
         with the dreadful
            reality
               that we
                  ought to be
                     perfect,
                 but we aren't.

And the most frustrating part
   is that
      THE HARDER WE TRY,
         THE WORSE IT GETS!
The harder I try to be "a TEN,"
   the more I work at being
      perfect,
         the more I realize
            that
               I'm not
               and
               NEVER
                  WILL BE . . .

It's like swimming *upstream*.
   But here we have it:

"*You*, therefore, must be
   perfect as your heavenly
      Father is perfect."
What, then, to do?

First, let me digress for a moment
into a little teaching by putting
this verse, this gospel reading,
into some context.

This is the fourth Sunday in a row
that we've had a reading
from the fifth chapter in
Matthew — each is part of
   the Sermon on the Mount,
   — thought of as the very
      heart and essence
         of Jesus' teachings —
            and the bedrock,
               therefore, of
                  the Christian faith.

It starts with the Beatitudes . . .
   those beautiful phrases,
      "Blessed are the poor in spirit . . ."
      ". . . the merciful . . ."
      ". . . the peacemakers . . ."

Then the images of salt and light . . .
   "You are the salt of the earth . . ."
   "You are the light of the world . . ."

Followed by Jesus' interpretation of
the Law.
   First he says of himself that he
   ". . . came not to abolish (the
   law and the prophets) but
   to fulfill them." Then he
   gives a number of examples
   of how he would interpret,
   or live out, the law.

— Which leads up to today's gospel lesson —
with its incredible, new approach.
   We are no longer to exact
   justice, nor even to resist evil.
   We are to "turn the other cheek"
   and *pray for* our enemies!

It's this new interpretation of
 the law that is so important —
  and it has a lot to do
   with perfection.

When we say "the Law," here, we mean
not only those basic principles laid
down in the Ten Commandments and
the Old Testament; "the Law" had
come to mean that AND the *rules*,
definition, and *commentary* about
how to keep the law.

The effort to keep all those detailed
rules was something like trying
to be perfect.

When Jesus said, then, that he came
NOT to abolish the law — but
by word and example *reinterpreted*
the law, he wasn't being inconsistent.
He was going back to the *heart*
of the law . . .
  to the greatest principles of
   REVERENCE and RESPECT.

Thus, he could say something like:
 "You've heard it said, an eye
  for an eye; but I say,
   turn the other cheek."

We tend, I think, to get hung
up in the legalities when we
hear these exhortations.
 But more than anything else,
  I believe Jesus was
   pointing toward —
    focusing on
     the inner life
      of the person.

Over and over again, Jesus is concerned
with the *thoughts* of people, with
their motives.

And he says: it's not enough to
just go through the motions —
 to outwardly keep the rules.

It must come from a
  genuine attitude of love.

For the Jews, righteousness
was the *result of* keeping the
law. ONE KEPT THE LAW IN ORDER TO BE RIGHTEOUS.
  Jesus seemed to say — NO —
    it's the other way around:
      Righteousness is a condition
        of the heart — an attitude —
          that *results* in
            being able to keep the
              law. ONE IS RIGHTEOUS
                IN ORDER TO KEEP THE LAW.

For the Jew, this was inconceivable.
  Just as it is inconceivable
    to us to be PERFECT.
We try to be perfect in order to love and be loved . . .
But it's the other way around.
When we *love* and *are loved*, we become perfect.

But nobody can just *be* righteous,
  just *be* perfect.
    So we come up with
      ways — rules — things
      we can measure —
        in order to try.

We lose touch with the heart of the matter —
with our inner selves — in our effort to
measure perfection/righteousness.

PERFECT (in the Greek, *telios*)
  means a number of things.
    — it means "faultless, without
      blemish" — as required for
      sacrificial animals.
        This is the meaning
          we usually get hung
            up on.
              But there are
                deeper meanings.

  — It also means to reach
      completion or fulfillment
        in the functional sense —

like a person who
has reached maturity
as opposed to being
a child,
like a student who
has mastered a subject
as compared to a beginner.

A thing is *telios* if it realizes the purpose
for which it was created.

We are *perfect* when we fulfill
the purpose for which we were
created.
Now that has individual
and unique implications
for each of us. But
if we get hung up
on the little things,
we will repeat
the error of the
Pharisees:
that is,
we will
get lost
in our
own efforts . . .
. . . and miss the heart of the matter.

In the broadest sense,
we — humankind — each of
us *and* all of us together
were created for one
purpose: to be the
image and likeness
of God.

Not in some abstract, philosophical,
theoretical way; no.
But in a simple way.
So Jesus says: just as God has
the sun to shine and
the rain to fall
on the
good and bad
alike,

. . . We are to love not only our
     dear ones, but also our enemies.

But if it is simple,
     it also seems overwhelming.
          How do we do such
               a thing
                    as love
                         that way?

I read a book recently about
     a little girl named Sheila.
          It was/is a true story
               of an abused, troubled child.

At the age of three, Sheila was abandoned
by her mother on a freeway;
she was left clinging to the guard
rail in the center median.
     Her itinerant father beat
     her regularly for
          misconduct.
               Sheila was an embittered,
               hostile, violent child —
               hopelessly locked into
               a pattern of trying to
               be perfect, failing
               miserably —
               proving that she was,
               therefore, unlovable —
               and continuing to
               believe that if she
               could somehow *do it
               right*, she would
                    be loved and her
                         mother would
                              come back.

It's a dramatic story,
     an exaggerated example —
          but not unlike
               our own.

We try so hard to be perfect,
     to do things right, to earn
          God's love and each other's.
          And we fail miserably.

Again and again
we fail to love
each other,
or to forgive,
or to be kind
or thoughtful.

And then we think:
If I could just
DO IT RIGHT
I would be loved.
WHEN I GET IT RIGHT,
I'll be happy.

But then Sheila met somebody different;
TOREY. And Torey didn't care
if she messed up. Torey didn't
mind if she made mistakes.

Torey even understood when
she cried . . . And cried . . .
. . . and cried.
She didn't have to be
perfect for Torey to love her.

The paradox — the healing paradox
was that slowly,
little by little,
Sheila became *free* to
be herself —
free to respond . . .
. . . and to give . . .
. . . and love back.

That's very much like the
PARADOX OF PERFECTION
for us.

The harder we try to make
ourselves perfect,
the more it's like swimming upstream;
the more self-defeating
it becomes.

The good news is this:
Being perfect as God is perfect
is THE RESULT of the
Grace of God.

Unlike any other faith,
  any other religion in
   history,
    ours depends
     not on our
      own efforts,
       but on the
        LOVE OF GOD.

We are enabled and empowered
  by God's Holy Spirit
   to respond, and to give, and
   to love.
    It is the gift of God,
     the Grace of God,
      given through
       Jesus.

But that is NOT to say that becoming
perfect is something God does TO us
without our consent.

It comes out of a relationship
with God.
  A sixth-century Christian
  named Dorotheoz (of Gaza)
  described it as sailing a
  ship; one works at the
  skill of sailing . . . while
   God is like the wind.
    It takes a *group*
     working together
     to sail a ship.
    The wind catches us up
    and carries us.

Our relationship with God can
be nurtured in a number
of ways, but especially *by prayer.*

And that's our reason for
coming here today.
  To be sure, we hear scripture,
   we listen to sermons, and we come
   for the fellowship.
   But most of all —
    to pray together.

Then we come
to the table
to receive the
Grace of God —

Empowering and enabling us
to respond, to give, and to love,
— To be perfect, even as God is perfect.

Being perfect isn't a struggle,
like swimming upstream.

The Paradox of Perfection
is being like Sheila —
letting ourselves be loved
in spite of our imperfection —
It is letting the love of
God flow through us,
enabling and empowering
us to respond,
to give, and to love —
in the likeness
and image of God.
Amen.

HOLY SATURDAY
Matthew 28:1-10

April 21, 1984
St. Bartholomew's Church
Atlanta, Georgia

At St. Bartholomew's we had been through Lent and the drama of Holy Week. Beginning with the turn of events on Palm Sunday, from "Hosanna" to "crucify him!" we had experienced Maundy Thursday and Good Friday. Holy Saturday, or Easter Eve, began with the lighting of the pascal candle and included Holy Baptism and the Eucharist. It was the first celebration of the Risen Christ.

As I prepared for the homily, I was aware of both practical matters and the theological and symbolic time. The practical agenda included the late hour (the service was at 11:00 p.m.) and the extended length of the service. I was occupied, also, with the feelings and experiences of the symbolic week and the anticipation of the Holy Saturday liturgy itself. The week had been full of the emotions of the Passion, and the Easter Eve service held the promise of celebration.

In my homily I wanted to rekindle the wonder of the story and, especially, to affirm the experiential aspect of the narrative. It did not seem to be the time to exegete the text or rationalize the resurrection. We who observe the church year liturgically are blessed with the opportunity to feel as well as to think. This, it seemed to me, was a time to feel.

This has been a week of drama and this has been a night for stories. We have heard tonight some of the stories of our tradition handed over to us across the centuries:

The Crossing of the Red Sea,
The Promise of Salvation,
The Empty Tomb.

And we have experienced throughout this week, the Christian Drama:

Palm Sunday
Maundy Thursday
Good Friday
and now. . . Holy Saturday . . .
the first celebration
of Easter.

Drama and stories — things expressly designed to be felt more than known,
It's the way we tell the most important things to our children . . .
the way we remember the most important events in
our lives.

When I was a small child, my beloved Granddaddy died. My mother held me in
her lap and told me . . .
Granddaddy's heart was sick, and when it just couldn't beat
anymore, the angels came and took him to heaven.

Stories sometimes push our rationality,
strain the intellect, but they tell the truth.

And at times when my own children have come to me with their
deepest questions, I have forgotten all the theories
of popular psychology and told them stories.

When we remember the dramatic events in our lives, we remember them in stories. Our parents told us stories of their courtships, of their travels, of their
friends. Family tragedies and celebrations alike are told and retold as stories.

My children never tire of hearing about each one's birth day.
What happened? How fast did you have to drive?
Where were you? What happened next?
What did I look like?

It's in the drama of our lives — and in the STORIES WE TELL ABOUT
THOSE DRAMAS, that we come to have an experience of who we
are . . . and of who the other is.

So tonight we have the ultimate story: JESUS, WHO WAS DEAD, IS NOW ALIVE!

As Christians . . . and by that I mean as folk born and raised in a Christian
culture, and most of us with some sort of church in our upbringing . . .
We Christians have a hard time really hearing the story.
We either pass over it quickly as if to say,
"Of course . . . "
OR
We come to some REASONABLE explanation that
satisfies our intellectual insecurities.

When I was in seminary, there was a man who had been raised Hindu, now a
Christian and studying for ministry. He would rush up to one of us or to a group
from time to time, absolutely incredulous at some part of the story he'd just read
in scripture. "LOOK AT THIS!" he would almost shout. "THIS IS WON-
DERFUL! DO YOU KNOW WHAT THIS SAYS!!??"
And almost with embarrassment, we would say . . .
"Yeah . . . right . . ."

But even if we can never hear the Story for the first time again, perhaps
we can still *FEEL* it.
That's why we tell it liturgically. Liturgy is a drama, a story told and
acted out *TO BE FELT.*

To feel the story is not to deny our intellect.
That, too, is a gift of God.
But to be a whole human being —
and the word WHOLE is from the same
root word as the word HOLY —
to be whole, is to develop the capacity to
feel as well as think.

HOW, though, can we experience THIS story?

It's an incredible story:
— a man, a teacher, preacher, healer,
put to death in the most ignominious manner —
naked, nailed, hung up in front of a crowd —
— his cold, dead body put in the arms of his grief-stricken
mother —
laid in a stone cave with a huge stone across the
entrance.
Then . . . ALIVE AGAIN?
Seen, touched, heard,
walked with by
his friends.

Is it too sentimental, too melodramatic to suggest that we put ourselves in the
story? Perhaps . . .

But if we can *FEEL* the story, it will tell us
who we are
and who God is.
It will tell us the truth.

GOD GRANT THAT WE MAY FEEL THE STORY. AMEN.

EASTER IV
John 10: 1-10

May 13, 1984
St. Bartholomew's Church
Atlanta, Georgia

It was with some hesitation that I included this sermon. The opening is dated and peculiar to a place and time. But sermons are like that, and I had hesitated before preaching it, too.

The first part is self-explanatory, noting a piece of parish business and a secular celebration. Sometimes one deals with these routine things from the pulpit. The parish knew I had been away at the Bethel training seminar, and it seemed important to acknowledge Mother's Day.

The real business of this sermon was John's gospel. Having studied and reflected at length on the meaning of "the abundant life," I concluded it is partly a by-product of risking really living and partly a state of being. It is not something easily described or pinned down; it is, in short, experimental. But how to convey that in a sermon? Somehow just to say it was to miss the mark.

When the idea of telling the puddle fish story first came to me, I rejected it. I had been told the story by a dear friend who was unavailable to confirm my memory of it; and I didn't know the source. But the more I thought of it, the more appropriate it seemed. After all, what is better than a story to evoke the closest thing to experience? Having committed myself thus far, I went "all the way" by changing modes in the middle of the sermon. From preaching, which for me is fairly straightforward talk, I went into an animated narration. I will always be grateful to the wide-eyed little girl in the third pew without whose rapt attention I could never have done it.

I am full of things to talk about this morning. I've been away on a trip, it's Mother's Day, and we have one of those great passages from the gospel of John. Too many things to talk about. I can't choose one to the total exclusion of the others, but neither can I talk all day. So I've had to do some difficult prioritizing.

First, a few words about my trip; because it will impact you, this parish. As many of you know, I've been at the Adult Christian Education Foundation in Madison, Wisconsin, for almost two weeks, preparing to launch the Bethel Bible Series here. This is a major undertaking for us. It has already required a large commitment of money and effort, and will now require an even greater commitment of *time* and effort. And it will be *your* program. *You* will be the teachers, and those of you who will be called to this task will prepare for *two years* before teaching it at the congregational stage.

I'm going to resist the urge to go into greater detail right now. But there will be a parish-wide mailing, a detailed letter of explanation, this week.

And then today is Mother's Day. You know, Mother's Day is a secular holiday, not part of the Christian calendar. The floral industry has created a real problem for those of us who preach from a lectionary; we can neither ignore something so important as Mother's Day, nor can we easily justify ignoring our texts for the day.

As a mother and as a daughter, I must say a few words about mothering, motherhood, and mothers. *We* who are mothers and *they* who are or were mothers DO THE BEST WE CAN. Sometimes it is woefully inadequate. Sometimes it is profoundly nurturing. So it was with mine, and so it is with me. And I suspect that, even as greatly as the church has venerated Mary, that she, too, was a *real* mother, and that her *mothering* of Jesus (as much as the fact of her birthing him) was part of his humanness.

So today we honor our mothers and celebrate mothering. I would like to suggest at the prayers that we each offer thanksgiving for our mothers, forgiving them for their failures, being grateful for their gifts to us.

Now . . . you've patiently followed me through two topics already. If this were a classroom, I'd give you a break before going on. But it's not, so take a deep breath and shift gears with me. I want to talk about John's gospel.

There are all kinds of interesting images of sheep and shepherds in this text and some other time I'll tell you about them. What I'm going to zero in on is the last phrase: (paraphrasing) "I came to give you life, and life abundantly."

"Abundant life" — that's one of our Christian catch-phrases. We've heard it most of our lives. At least, I have. And yet, what does it mean? What is the abundant life? Is it a promise of prosperity, wealth, ease, gracious living? Is it a promise of health, comfort, long life?

Those explanations are hard to square. Here we are, the gathered faithful, and some of us are poor, some of us are struggling to make ends meet. Some of us are struggling with emotional issues and personal relationships. Some of us are sick, and some of us have lost innocent, young loved ones.

What then is the abundant life?

In reading one of those books that preachers dig around in while preparing sermons, I ran across a comment about John's understanding of *life*. It said that to John, *life* means to *share in the life of God*. At first I just passed over that as one of those abstract things that theologians are always saying. But the more I thought about it, the more it began to dawn on me —

What could be more abundant than
to share in the life of God?

A clue, I thought!
But then . . . what do we
know about the life of God?
Actually, nothing. We
don't know anything
about the life of God.

But what we *do* know is what we
see *of* and *about* God in creation.
God's own creation tells us about God.
It tells us that there is light and
dark; there is order and
chaos; there are miracles
and disasters.
There is joy and there is grief.

We could go on and on . . . describing
the paradoxes of life. So what does
that tell us about the ABUNDANT life?

Well, I think it tells us this:
that the abundant life,
the life which is shared
life with God —
is one that is lived
in an incredible, vital,
life-giving kind of
TENSION.

It is to both lean headlong into life,
and to savor it *slowly;*
to be eager . . . and to wait.
To trust and to be skeptical,
Give and receive,
Hold onto and let go,
Celebrate and grieve.

It is NOT to live life wrecklessly,
with no limits or lines,
but it is to be open and spontaneous
and to respond to the moment.

And most of all, it is to risk loving,
and that is the greatest risk of all.

But how are we to bear it? How do
we know what to do?

Rules and answers,
   the safe and the familiar
      would be *so* much easier!

Once upon a time
   there was a puddle alongside
     a river. And in the puddle
      lived some puddle fish.
       They lived there very
       comfortably, swimming
       around in circles, eating
       waterbugs.

Then one day — out of nowhere — a huge, beautiful golden fish landed — splash — in the middle of their puddle.

Terrified . . . all the little puddle fish scurried under the roots of the tree that surrounded their puddle. And they watched and waited, shivering with fear.

Then the beautiful, golden fish began to swim around a little, saying, "It's all right. I won't hurt you. What do you *do* here?"

One brave little puddle fish ventured out a little way and explained, "We live here. This is our puddle. We swim around in circles and eat waterbugs."

"Oh," said the golden fish, "don't you know about the sea?" "What's the sea?" asked another puddle fish.

"The sea," said the golden fish, "is out there. It's so big that you can't see the end of it. And it's so full of things that you can never count them all!"

Well now, the puddle fish paused to consider all this new information. Shortly, one swam out and said flatly, "No such thing!"

Then after an embarrassed pause – because puddle fish don't like rudeness — another swam out to say, "Well, of course, we're all quite sure that the sea is quite real to *you*. We are, after all, open-minded puddle fish."

Then another ventured to ask, "Where *is* the sea and *how does* one get to it?"

And the big, golden fish said this: "It's at the end of the river. And all you have to do is swim around and around very fast, and *jump* over this bank, into the river, and the river will carry you into the sea."

"But the river has swift currents and snags along the edges!" exclaimed the puddle fish.

"Yes," said the golden fish, "but the river will carry you along and it's the only way to get to the SEA. And soon this puddle will be gone. The rain won't come and it will dry up. But the river will take you to the SEA!"

Just then, another puddle fish swam out to suggest reasonably, "Why don't we establish a *group* to study this matter? We could meet once a week to discuss the dangers of the river and this . . . SEA."

There was a pause for a moment. And then the golden fish said, "No," and then slowly began to swim around in a circle. Each time around, it went a little faster. At first, all the puddle fish just watched. But then one swam out and began to swim around with the golden fish, going faster and faster. And in a little while, two more puddle fish began to circle with them, and then another. They swam faster and faster . . . and then *leaped* over the edge of the puddle into the river!"

For awhile, all the other little puddle fish just hovered there in the roots. But soon they began to swim out, and they swam slowly around the puddle, until the water settled down. And it wasn't long at all until they were eating waterbugs again.

Amen.

The Reverend Doris Graf Smith

I realized in the midst of marriage and having children that I would never be happy at home full-time. Before my second child was born, I had quit teaching English and math. During the next several years, I did various things which allowed me to be home as much as possible but still do some writing, organizing, and planning. I even entered law school for a year.

When it became clear that I needed to settle somewhere, I discovered that everything I was interested in doing required more schooling. I could not imagine this after the law school experience. The disruption to the family and to the marriage had been overwhelming; I had quit to preserve both.

But God has a way of installing new vision. At the same time I very timidly let myself admit I wanted to seek holy orders, my attorney husband began meeting weekly with three other professionals to talk about their spiritual journey and about themselves. Through this he began to see that things could change at home and still be tolerable, if not perfect. Together, we struggled with my decision. At the end of the "Experiment in Ministry" year (which is a year of intense reflection about suitability for ordained ministry), we were able to break new ground together as I set off to seminary.

I have a love-hate relationship with preaching. I love to write and to create, but hate the time and the anguish.

I start my exegetical work at least a week before the sermon. I refer to six scholars whose work I trust. If I still feel at odds with the texts, I go to the library for research. I have four preaching resources which I read. Sometimes I start with a sermon suggestion, but before the process is over, I have often left that behind for something which fits me, my experience, and my congregation's better.

I suspect I use images because I think that way, a frustrated painter, maybe. I also am a frustrated pianist, so I sometimes find I make music with words, too. My experiences generally stay with me, and I use them. I'm not nearly organized enough to keep a file card or notebook, although, in my next life, I'm sure I will be more disciplined and will attend to this.

I used to compose longhand; now I can only compose at a typewriter. I think my mind runs too fast for a pencil. The way I put the sermon on paper is the way I dictate through the typewriter. I keep trying to outline first; when I do, the writing goes faster. But, the truth is, I don't usually know where I'm going until I get there. On the journey, though, is often where I meet God again. I guess that's worth the trip.

ADVENT IV
Isaiah 7:10-17
Romans 1:1-7
Matthew 1:18-25

December 18, 1983
St. Anne's Church
Atlanta, Georgia

This sermon was preached at St. Anne's Espiscopal Church. St. Anne's is in the affluent northwest section of Atlanta and has about 1,000 members.

This fourth Sunday of Advent fell on December 18th. The calendar said Advent, but most of us were deep into Christmas. The first issue was to own this. As I thought of some way to do this, the ballet idea came to mind.

Since I had done an Advent Bible study class, I had already done the exegetical work on the gospel. I was able to spend most of my study time on Isaiah. I became interested in the conflict between Ahaz and Isaiah. This became a natural way to introduce the idea of "God with us."

The next part of the sermon happened as I asked myself to answer the question, "Why would God want to be with us?" The illustration about the cans of food occurred two days before the sermon and was fresh on my mind. The insight about Jesus' birth into the human family was given to me by Ted Hackett in a sermon he preached in chapel at Candler School of Theology.

I enjoyed writing and preaching this sermon. The parish responded to it with warmth and with their own reasons for sometimes fleeing from Christmas. God was with us that day, too.

To all God's beloved who are called to be saints;
Grace to you and peace from God our Father and the Lord Jesus Christ.
Amen.

This fourth Sunday in Advent feels a little like a memory I have from
years ago,
when I opened the stage door before a ballet performance.
Everyone was busy getting ready. . .
a hectic pace of stagehands and dancers
warming up,
moving props,
being excited.

The performance was much later that night,
    but the activity had begun,
        and I got a glimpse of what was about to happen.

Today, we open the stage door just a little
    on the joyous remembrance and celebration of our Lord's birth into
        time and space.

But also today, we look back through that door,
    back even beyond the manger
    and the dream Joseph had.
Back 2700 years ago to a man of wealth —
    a man who was at home in the palaces of kings —
        a man who heard a call from God to take a message into the world.
            We call him a prophet . . . his name is Isaiah.

When Isaiah was called by God, he felt inadequate; felt unclean;
    perhaps afraid;
        But he also felt God's forgiveness and affirmation.
            He responded to God's call with those solid words,
                "Here I am, send me."

This Old Testament lesson this morning is the story of one of those
    times when Isaiah went forth to carry God's message.

The King of the southern part of Judah
    was named Ahaz.

Ahaz had a problem.
    The territories around Judah had aligned against him.
        It looked as if his kingdom would collapse.
            And there was terror in the heart of Ahaz.
                The King was ready to make a deal with the emperor
                to save the country.

When Isaiah came to Ahaz,
    the two men were separated by a gulf of conflicting concerns,
        Ahaz was worried about immediate doom;
            Isaiah was concerned that Ahaz had stopped looking to God
                for deliverance.

So Isaiah, speaking as the Lord, told Ahaz to ask for a sign from God —
    a sign that would tell him what would happen.

But Ahaz didn't want to trust that and would not ask for a sign.

To this the prophet responded,
    You will be given a sign anyway!
        "Behold a young woman shall conceive and bear a son, and shall
        call his name Immanuel."

This son will live when the kingdoms you fear are no more . . .
    the terror will go away from the land.
Ahaz, you need not concern yourself about the moral problems going
    on inside your country.

But Ahaz did not want to hear all this.
    He went his own way, and his lands were swallowed up.
    They became subservient to the powerful Assyrian empire.

What Isaiah told Ahaz was to trust God, but Ahaz chose to trust an
    earthly military power instead.
Ahaz could not hear
and would not listen to Isaiah's reality; *God was with Ahaz.*

Isaiah could trust that reality.
    He knew it.
        He had experienced it.
        and he spent his life telling it to the people.

When we cut through all history,
    all the wars and pestilence,
        the fears and sorrows,
            the core of what we are about is those very words . . .
            GOD IS WITH US.

Incredible isn't it?
    Why would God even want to be with us?
        I suspect that question is one of the reasons the Christmas season
        has sometimes been so overwhelming to me.
            There is something very heavy about receiving the gift of God's
            Son . . .
                being given a sign of that love . . .
                reminded again that God sent God's son into our world.

I suspect this may be one of the reasons I have sometimes tried
    to hype myself up to some great peak of frenzy,
        with presents and parties and decorations —
        to an extreme . . .
        wanting to find a way to run from the reality of that love.

Sometimes, I've gone the other route and discounted the whole enterprise,
    sneaking into the stores to buy my gifts . . .
        devoutly angry that the season has gone so commercial . . .
        wanting . . . could it be? . . . to sneak through the
        days of December, the days of preparation,
            without letting the reality of GOD IS WITH US
            sink in.

Why would God want to be with us?
 We who plunder the creation;
  who wage war on poverty often slaying the poor as we go;
  we who do not listen to the signs;
  who do not trust;
   we who are sinners.

The only answer I know is,
 GOD CHOSE TO BE WITH US
 to create us, to guide us, to love us.

And while we can run from that,
 we cannot change that for God, even as God was with Ahaz, will not
 relent; will not be pushed forever aside; will not let us forget that
 God loves that which is God's creation.

There comes into our view through the stage door gently opening . . .
 the story of a baby . . .
  who would be born to Mary . . .
and a man whose name is Joseph . . .
 who would care for the child
 protect him . . .
  give him a home . . .
   and even teach him a trade . . .

When Matthew wrote his gospel story . . .
 he wrote to tell all who would listen . . .
  that GOD IS WITH US.
 Matthew knew Isaiah's words . . .
  that a son would be born . . .
  and he knew of the ministry of Jesus . . .
  and of his death . . .
   and of his resurrection . . .
   Matthew knew in full
    what Isaiah knew in part

And so Matthew wrote his gospel
 not as a prophet who told of things to come . . .
  but as a believer beyond the empty tomb . . .
  he wrote to tell us what we already know . . .
   God came to us . . .
    to bear our sins for us . . .
    to be with us.

"Joseph, son of David, do not fear to take Mary
 your wife, for that which is conceived in her
 is of the Holy Spirit . . .
  she will bear a son . . .
  and you shall call his name Jesus
   for he will save his people from their sins . . .

All this took place to fulfill what the Lord had spoken to the
   prophet . . .
     Behold, a virgin shall conceive and bear a son,
      and his name shall be called Emmanuel
       which means God with us . . ."
Joseph, Matthew tells us . . .
   responded in faith to God's sign
   and took Mary home.
     Joseph did not turn away . . .
      he faithfully accepted the message that God was with him . . .

We come to this fourth Sunday of Advent . . .
   the products of thousands of years of testimony
    that God is with us.
And we come too with a thousand different thoughts
   and feelings . . .
 Some of us unsure of just what it is we are supposed to
  be feeling . . .
Some pensive because we know next year we will
  be in a new place . . . a new town . . . a new job . . .
  and we will not be here . . .
Some of us come home trying to fit back into a family we have left.
Some of us come utterly excited as we wait for the
  big day and all the family and presents to be
   enjoyed . . .
Some angry that so much is being asked of us
  right now and the burden seems heavy

And we cannot run from these feelings either . . .
  we can only take time to know that
   God is with us in the midst of wherever we are . . .

On Friday morning . . .
  I flipped on the TV
   to watch the Today program . . .
    only the Today program wasn't on . . .
     the Eleven Alive Can-A-Thon
     was being broadcast . . .

The cans of food
  were being brought
   to places in Atlanta and Athens and Rome . . .
    and as I watched the kids and the workers . . .
     the choirs and the cars . . .
      my eyes filled up with tears . . .

I don't usually cry watching tin cans . . .
  ordinary tin cans . . .

cans of greens and peas . . .
or corn and beans . . .
but I cried Friday morning . . .
They were tears of gratitude
because I was moved by this expression of
the good in us . . .
the good that does not know what
to do with all the suffering in the world . . .

And so we risk at Christmas
a tin can of tuna
to feed a hungry person.
As the people drove up and gave away their bags of cans . . .
I thought yes, it is hard to understand
and yet sometimes we do,
God loves us,
God gave us a Savior . . .
and give him to the world
into a human family . . .
The same God who knows the world does not know
very well how to love . . .
knows we do try to love . . .
and into that human love
God trusted
to send The Savior as
a baby to be held and loved.

God loves us so much
to give us a prophet . . .
to give us the story . . .
to give us each other to bring cans of
food and pints of blood . . .
It is in the good that God brought to us . . .
the good that God will not let us forget in us . . .
that we also have as a sign that *God is* with us . . .

And so as we crack open the stage door . . .
especially now . . .
this week before . . .
in the midst of the commotion and the confusion
and in the midst of the aloneness . . . and maybe
we see more clearly what we have always known . . .
the Jesus who came to bear our burdens
comes to show us why God loves us . . .

We are God's people . . .
  and so God is with us . . .
    we need not be afraid . . .
      nor be ashamed . . .
        or feel unclean . . .
          we need rather . . .
            to *own* our faith . . .
              God sent us a sign . . .
                Come, let us worship.

                  In the name of the
                  Father, and of the
                  Son and of the
                    Holy Spirit . . . Amen.

May 13, 1984
St. Anne's Church
Atlanta, Georgia

There was little way to avoid shepherd thinking on a day with the theme so clearly picked. I was just finishing a semester's work in pastoral care and had spent many hours reading about shepherding as a pastoral care tool. But I kept thinking that sheep and shepherds are not part of our everyday life experience. I needed to build a foundation with the congregation if the real power of the shepherd was to have current day meaning. Somewhere in my recent reading, I came across some history of the shepherd in Palestine. As I recalled that, things began to click, so I set out to wrench away the quiet scene of the shepherd on the verdant hillside.

The next step was to connect ourselves to being sheep and shepherds. The best way for me to do this was to go with the reverse. (Perhaps since I was in the middle of final exams, I could easily get in touch with facing fierce wild lions.) John's gospel became the outline for the rest of the sermon. I wanted to draw a picture of the shepherd John talked about and then try to create some ways we could experience being sheep under that leadership. The conclusion which came to me at the end of this sermon was the one I spoke of in my introductory comments, for this was a time when I felt God had given me an insight which helped me know the Christ and myself better: Sheep and shepherd being both strong and vulnerable, another mysterious paradox of being a Christian.

L ong years ago, a young man stood before a King and gave this description of himself . . .

"Your majesty, I take care of my father's sheep. Any time a lion or a bear carries off a lamb, I go after it, attack it, and rescue the lamb. And if the lion or bear turns on me, I grab it by the throat and beat it to death. The Lord has saved me from lions and bears; he will save me from this Philistine."

The book of First Samuel gives us this as an early description of a shepherd.

For David . . . being a shepherd meant to have courage . . .
   to be strong . . .
      to want to protect the lamb from being
         carried away and killed.

His courage to take care of the sheep became courage to face a giant . . .
   and his faith in God stood with him in both.

Many paintings we see of shepherds
    show a rather delicate figure far removed from the hardiness and physical
        courage of the shepherds who actually walked the Palestinian
            hills and valleys . . .
                who were often lonely as they searched in
                    the dry season for a green pasture,
                        a place to rest . . .
                            a spring to drink from.

The shepherd had to be dedicated . . . powerful . . . and have that extra
    sense to know what was best for the flock.
        His job was to walk the hills . . .
            to lead . . . to nurture . . . to heal . . . to bring the scattered
                flock back together . . .

Images of what it was to be a shepherd fill the pages of the Old and
    the New Testaments . . .
        Listen to how the Prophet Ezekiel describes God as
            Shepherd . . .

"I myself will be the shepherd of my sheep, and I will make them lie down,
    says the Lord God. I will seek the lost, and I will
        bind up the crippled, and I will strengthen the weak, and
            the fat and the strong I will watch over;
                I will feed them justice."
Present, caring, and *able* are the images connected to God as Shepherd
    of the people.
    And it was shepherds who were in the region keeping
        watch over their flocks by night . . .
            whom the angels came to the night our Lord was born . . .
                who heard the call and went to Bethlehem to see
                    what the Lord had made known to them.

Jesus uses the shepherd image in his own teaching as another way
    to describe God's love . . . .
        Of course, there is the story of the 99 sheep who are left by
            the shepherd because one is lost . . . and the keeper
                of the flock who goes to find the lost one . . .

It is joy which abounds when that one is found . . . and the flock is
    together again!

In the verse which follows our Gospel reading today,
    Jesus names himself the Good Shepherd saying . . .
        "I am the Good Shepherd.
            The Good Shepherd lays down his life for his sheep."

It is the final image of the one who walks the land with the
flock . . . the image of sacrifice.

But what are we to make of all this?
Is it reasonable, in any way, to think of ourselves . . .
the sophisticated, nuclear folks that we are, to
think of ourselves as being ones who still need
a shepherd?

There are no more giants who need to be slain — Are There?

And surely with our technology and independence,
we do not need ever to be lost . . .
How can anyone get lost with cordless telephones
on sale in every Eckerd's drugstore . . .
with beepers that will chase us down . . .
(even during a church service . . .)
let alone all the computer terminals
with our checking account numbers . . .
our credit ratings . . . and
our last payment to Neiman-Marcus
ready to be printed at the
touch of a finger?

Are there still lost among us who need a shepherd?
If there were, then we would have to be something like those sheep
who moved on the heights and down into the shadowy
valleys in Palestine . . .
sometimes errantly wandering off,
getting caught in a thorn bush,
being chased by a fierce wild lion,
falling prey to whatever led us off the path.

We would be those who need to be nurtured,
who need someone to hang in there with us,
to be for us,
to call us by name so we know whose flock we belong to.

We would be those who need a guide who leads us to green pastures . . .
and who with tender strength hangs tough with us through the
dry seasons.
Who would lay down his life for us.

Do you suppose *we* could need to receive a part of the letter Peter wrote
those early Christians . . . ?
to be told . . . reminded . . . that it is by the wounds of the one
who names himself the Good Shepherd that we have been
healed . . . ?

Would it be so bad to be a sheep in such a flock?
> To have as a shepherd one who above all else has courage
>> *For* others . . . who never tries to take over all the power
>>> offered him? Who can call down a hated tax collector
>>> and go to his house and eat with him?

To belong to a flock whose shepherd stands calmly before the Sanhedrin
> and faces death? Who accepts the tears of a prostitute as
> a gift of love?
>> Who lets a doubting follower named Thomas thrust his hands
>> into the shepherd's sides?
>>> A shepherd who will eat with a man who is about
>>> to betray him?

A shepherd whose words . . . whose actions . . . whose sufferings are all
courageous? Would this be so bad?

But there is something unique in being a sheep in this flock . . .
> Being a sheep also means learning how to be a shepherd —
>> Through a power most mysterious, most holy,
>>> taking on some of the *courage* and the *tender strength*
>>> of the Great Shepherd . . .
>>>> It means standing by while others in the flock are in
>>>> the shadows . . .
>>>> in the valleys . . .
>>>>> lost . . .
>>>>> with giants and lions closing in.

Can we be both sheep and shepherds?
> Can we be wounded healers?

To be a shepherd means being willing to go into the loneliness . . .
> to trust our own worth . . . our own ability to lead . . .
>> to hang in there when people disappoint us
>>> and wander off after we've tried so hard to show
>>> them the right way.

It means weeping in the night because someone got away . . .
> and then finding courage to still hold watch and call her or his name
> in the dark .

Sometimes shepherds look famous like Dr. Martin Luther King or
> Sister Teresa.
>> Sometimes a shepherd looks like a little league coach . . .
>>> sometimes a spouse who stands by when the other wants to
>>> change careers.

Shepherds can look like mothers and fathers who find ways to
> get their children through college and stand with them
>> as they grow into adulthood . . .
>>> or teenagers who work hard to get the youth program

alive again in their parish church . . . or a business person who speaks
> to a colleague about a drinking problem.

And sometimes shepherds are grandparents who answer the other
   end of a phone ready to talk or listen or come
     be with a child who needs them.

    They come in all ages . . .
      in all types of dress . . .

And I suspect each of you can name a time when you have been
   a shepherd . . .
     willing to be there for another sheep . . .
      maybe even for one who has in another time
      been shepherd for you.

Can a sheep ever really be a full-time shepherd?
   Probably not . . . not like the one who leads our flock . . .
    not just exactly like the Good Shepherd . . .
     but there is room in this world for lesser shepherds
     who know what it is to be loved —
      that they can risk the valleys
       and climb the ridges . . .
        and hang tough in the in-between.

The shepherd we can be will always be sometimes shepherd
   and sometimes sheep . . .
     moving in and out.

We can come to know the strength of our shepherding as we see those who
   follow us, finding rest and health . . .
     — finding, in turn, their own ways to become shepherds.

And we will know something of the courage we have as shepherds
   as we risk ourselves . . .
     even when that costs us and is terribly dangerous . . .
     when we let our sheep wounds show . . .
      so someone else can be healed.

Jesus says to us, "I came that they may have life, and have it abundantly."

I have a notion that the *abundant* life our Lord speaks of
   is a life wherein we are both *sheep* and *shepherd* . . .
    a life lived heeding the voice of the keeper
    of the flock . . .
     knowing *him* as our *true* Good Shepherd . . .
Knowing ourselves to be a sheep of his own flock
   a sinner of his own redeeming . . .
    and then *in* this,
     by Him and *with* Him and *in* Him
      through the power of the Holy Spirit . . .
      finding ourselves
       shepherds, too. Amen.

PENTECOST III
Isaiah 2:10-17
Romans 6:3-11
Matthew 10:34-42

July 1, 1984
St. Bartholomew's Church
Atlanta, Georgia

This sermon was written for my home parish. It is both alpha and omega, since it was my first there as an ordained minister and my last there for the foreseeable future. St. Bartholomew's is a suburban parish with a mix of people. While I knew many of them, there were also many new faces.

As I studied the propers, the lessons for the day seemed incongruous with each other and with the carefree feel of a summer in Atlanta. I needed to untangle this to address the sermon. The idea of ordinary time came to mind, and, with that, the reflection on what it means to be a disciple day to day. It is incongruous to be a Christian in the world. Once I got in touch with the paradoxes of such living, the other images came.

Grace and peace from God our Father and the Lord Jesus Christ.

To come home is always a special treat. You are home for me. This is the
place wherein I began to grow up . . .
even though I was 21 when I first came here.
These are the walls I pushed against as I sought to find
out about an adult relationship with our Lord.
This is the table where I was fed and sustained.
Your ideas have gone with me to the other
parishes I have served . . . your vision
has served well as it has been shared
with others . . .
You are the people who sustained me as I
tried my wings long before any thoughts
of ever being a priest entered my
conscious mind. It was in this
place I first chanced the word
that ordained ministry was
what I felt called to do.
You have hung with me. . .
been constant in your
support . . . and a

continued home place for my family as I moved about
    on the pilgrimage toward ordination . . .

You are special people . . .
    My family in Christ.
        It is a privilege to come home one more time.

Having said that, it is time to turn to the matter at hand . . .
    the lessons for today.
        At first glance, these lessons seem to be misplaced!
            In fact, I even looked them up to see if they in fact
                were repeats from Lent.
There is a somberness about them,
    almost a foreboding,
        a seriousness that seems out of place during the
            carefree months of summer.

I have been out of town for several weeks
    and had taken my material with me . . .
        hoping to prepare the sermon before I returned . . .
But I didn't manage that . . .
    I wrote some things . . .
        but when I returned and really got down to the sermon . . .
            I realized that one could not deal with these lessons
                on an airplane.
Their call to us is profound . . . both serious and complex.

Listen to the words in the Old Testament again for a moment . . .
    "Enter into the rock
        and hide in the dust . . .
            from before the terror of the Lord
                and from the glory of his majesty."

terror and majesty . . .
    don't we know the truth of that?
        the naked reality
            spoken in those lines?
                for God is a great God . . .
                    and God's power and God's majesty
                        call us to confront our life
                            with both fear and awe.

(I, however, rather prefer to do my serious religious thinking
    during Lent . . . and perhaps during Holy Week.)
But here we are on the first of July . . .
    It is interesting that these long weeks after Pentecost
        in the Roman Catholic church are not designated as
            whichever Sunday after Pentecost . . .

They are rather referred to as ordinary time . . .
   The Sundays of the earth . . .
     the regular days of the year.
And on these ordinary days we are told the ordinary way we are
   expected to exist as Christians
     people on a pilgrimage from life to life . . .
       in that ordinary time between the
        already and the not yet . . .
         between baptism and glory.

It is during the ordinary Sundays that we are instructed
   in the reality of discipleship . . .
     instructed, however, along side the reality that the *Holy*
      Spirit is present to sustain us along the way.
       During these days we are reminded of the *totality*
        of the *day to day* call to
         discipleship.
Perhaps this is why the church does not put these lessons
   into the lectionary during festival times
     when the church is filled with those who come
       only to feel good . . .
these are the words which come to us not to comfort . . .
   but to challenge . . .
     to make us wholly aware that we are called
       daily to take up the cross of devotion
        and follow the one who hung on a cross.

Gone from view is the gentle Jesus of the manger.
   Today the gospel words arch the spine . . .

And Jesus said . . . "Do not think that I have come to bring peace
   on earth; I have not come to bring peace, but a sword.
     For I have come to set man against his father, and a daughter
       against her mother, and a daughter-in-law
        against her mother-in-law."

These are words that ask for something total . . .
   warning us that whatever stands between ourselves and Christ
     is a separation that cannot be tolerated,
for . . . to use St. Paul's understanding . . .
   all of us who have been baptized into Christ Jesus were
     baptized into his death.
We were buried, therefore, with him by baptism into death, so
   that as Christ was raised from the dead by the glory of the Father,
     we too might walk in the newness of life . . .
Our old self crucified with him so that the sinful body might be
   destroyed. If we have died with Christ, we believe
     that we shall also live with him.

There is nothing here which speaks of compromise . . .
   there is nothing here sentimental.

Either we die with Christ . . . or we don't
   either Christ is first . . .
     or Christ is nothing.

Oh come on Doris, you might say, aren't you pushing it a bit?

If you think this is comfortable for me . . .
   we've been apart too long!

But think about it . . .
   what happens when we fall headlong in love with someone or something?
     does it matter what friends think?
       does it matter that parents don't approve?
        when we love someone or something
         we move toward that person or thing
          with all the energy and devotion we know . . .
often with energy and devotion we did not even know we had . . .
   we go forward
     and that person or thing becomes for us the
       most important entity in all the world.
Hang the rest of creation . . .
   it's me and him . . .
     or you and her . . .
       or me and it . . .
        and nothing separates.

It strikes me that just as Christ knows the ways of sinners —
   knows our weaknesses . . .
     our needs,
       just as he could understand Peter and Thomas and Mary,
       he also understands the ways of the heart . . .
       and knows that unless we can love him with total
        devotion . . .
         a devotion which will cleave us unto him . . .
          against all the words of whomever or whatever that
          would separate us from him . . .
           unless we know that kind of love . . .
            we cannot take seriously the reality
            that we must die with him
            giving up our old selves
Not letting ourselves be lured by the sinful world . . .
   but striving daily to take up our cross and follow Christ Jesus.

This must be our ordinary life . . . day by day.

Perhaps many of us can recall some time when we have loved in this way . . .
when we moved toward someone or something. . .
when we possessed that special zeal. . .
when nothing was impossible . . .
when challenges were met with incredible energy and
conviction . . .
when the simple beauty of a sunset was enough to make us tingle —
a time when no one and no thing could separate us from that
person or cause or thing which we loved.

But, dear friends, that is being "in love"
and being "in love" *is wonderful* and *awful* —
it is a total experience . . .
The only problem is that no one can sustain being "in love"
forever . . . after being "in love" there comes the *ordinary* time —
and it is during this ordinary time when the real
value of the relationship is tested.

But didn't I just say that what we are called to do is to have the
single-minded devotion which we might have experienced when
we were "in love"?

Yes, I think I did . . .
well, then, what is this rubbish about?

Any of us who have had a conversion experience . . . if we are
far enough away from it . . .
have lived through those dark days when the incredible
high became the incredible low.

Life becomes most ordinary again . . .
the sunset is just the end of another day. . .
and the other day just a repetition of the worries and problems
of the day before.

To use a well-known phrase . . .
the honeymoon is over.

Enter the sword.
The peace falls away . . . but the sword lingers.

This is where we are . . .
here today in the ordinary time,
the time when the metal of our devotion is called to the fore.
Will we be able to find the strength to take up our cross
and follow after him when doing that has lost its romantic ardor?
Can we even believe that such a journey is worthwhile?

Have you ever been with a couple who has survived the honeymoon?
   survived years and years of being with each other
      through good and bad . . .
         who have somehow worn old together . . . worn old loving each other?
   Have you ever been there toward the end of their lives
      and seen love that is so strong
         that it sustains them through illness and into death?
            when their frail bodies are strong as a sword?
               where they whack away at fear
                  and though they do not coo over each other . . .
                     are there . . . strong as flint . . . for each other . . .
                     caring and loving?

They seem unaware of the totality of their devotion . . .
   it is so commonplace for them . . .
      yet the outsider is touched by the intimacy
         between them as one spoons soup into the frail
            mouth of the other . . .
               Looking on, the visitor feels almost like a "peeping Tom" watching
                  the gentle touch of his hand on the sheet as it
                  is pulled higher to warm her as she
                    feels the chill of death.

These people have turned the *ordinary* into the *deepest kind* of
   loving relationship . . . they have lost a sense of themselves
      into a sense of the other . . . yet they are each their
         own persons . . .
            they have *lived together* so long . . .
               talked with each other so much . . .
                  that they are *united* in the realness
                    of their *joined* lives.
   And nothing can separate them one from the other.
   This is, I believe, what we are being called to participate in
      today. Not to be just "in love" with Christ . . .
         But to love him . . .
            to forsake comfort and ease . . .
               success and fortune . . .
                  even family if that is the price . . .
                  to grow old loving him . . . to grow old with *him*.

To come to him and speak *to* him . . . and speak *of* him,
   to be his voice and to be his touch in a lonely hostile world
to slash with a sword of truth and love and devotion the
      evil which abounds —

He calls us into his death, so we can sustain the reality of life.
   He calls us to feel *death swallow us alive*
      so that the life we live becomes life *in him*.

In our baptisms we are given the grace to die . . .
  — given the *grace* to die —
    to be emptied of sin
      to become heirs of eternal life . . .
        to become a part of the eternal
          order . . .
        the *ordinary* of God's creation.
When I was little, my mother would often say to me as I would leave
  her to go somewhere . . .
    "Remember who you are, Doris, and act that way."

Who are we? Not peaceful insipid souls.
  No, we are called and named to be sword carriers —
    to follow a crucified Lord.
We are forgiven sinners who are loved by a *terribly majestic* God
    who is with us *in* the ordinary
    and who is with us *into* eternity.

"Give me your life," our Lord says.
  Give me your life for I have given you mine.
    Give me your life, and I will give you my sword of peace.
      Give me your life, and I will help carry your burdens.
        Give me your life and your love, and
          I will wash your weary feet.
In your baptism you were joined into my death . . .
  Now join me in my life —
    know me . . .
      trust me . . .
        for whoever loses his or her life for my sake will find it.

Amen.

Barbara Brown Taylor

It was almost ten years after my first day in seminary that I was ordained a deacon in the Episcopal church on June 11, 1983. Now that I know where those years led, all their turns and reversals make sense to me. The living of them was something else altogether, a decade spent learning the design of an intricate maze.

I arrived at Yale Divinity School in the fall of 1973 on a Rockefeller Trial Year in Seminary fellowship, which allowed me one free year at the seminary of my choice. I had applied for the grant less out of a sense of call than of curiosity — it was at that time an eccentric idea for a woman to go to seminary, which appealed to me. If I claim one guiding principle for my life, it is to say yes to unusual propositions and see what happens.

What happened first at Yale was that I felt grievously out of place. Surrounded by high achievers spouting theological jargon and already cramming for their ordination exams, I felt lightweight and lost. I did not even belong to a church. Christened Roman Catholic, I had spent time in Methodist, Episcopal, and

Unitarian Sunday schools, had been baptized for the second time when I joined the Baptist church at 16, had been saved repeatedly by the Navigators at Emory, and was active at the Catholic student center before settling into the interdenominational community that worshipped at the university's chapel.

I did not know what an exegesis was and had no idea of the difference between Barth and Tillich. By my second semester, however, I had begun to get the hang of divinity school and decided to keep my options open. After talking briefly with the Methodists, I joined Central Presbyterian Church in Atlanta because it was the most socially active congregation in the city.

I do not remember even considering the Episcopal church. The ordination of women was not yet legal, of course, but my avoidance went deeper than that. In the unlikely event that I were ordained, I thought, I could never think of myself as a priest. A woman minister, yes, a woman pastor, certainly, but not a woman priest. The words would not go together in my head.

But as luck or fate or the will of God would have it, the Episcopal church was where I finally landed, influenced by a strong Anglican community at Yale and drawn by the exquisite liturgy at Christ Church, New Haven. Through the rector of that parish, David Boulton, I fell in love with the history, theology, and ethos of the Episcopal church; and I saw someone I wanted to be like. After more than a year's worth of weekly instruction with him, I was confirmed at Easter 1976, just weeks before graduation.

I still did not intend to be ordained. Everything I learned in seminary had taught me that the power and future of the church belonged to the ministry of the laity, and that was where I wanted to take my stand. While I tried to figure out how exactly to do that, I moved back to Atlanta and took a job at Emory's Candler School of Theology. I also began attending St. Luke's Church, where Tom Bowers was rector, and eventually joined the church staff as part-time lay pastoral assistant.

It was through that work — assisting at the liturgy, visiting the sick and elderly, teaching and preaching – that I began to change my mind about ordination. I do not know whether it was my call or my own desire, but I began to recognize how much I wanted a ministry that included preaching and the sacraments. I went to see the bishop and found out about the Experiment in Ministry, the Diocese of Atlanta's vocational testing program. It was expensive in both money and time, with no guarantee of ordination at the end. I thought about it for a year.

I finally entered the program in 1979 and was recommended for postulancy a year later, but with the requirement of a second year's training, this time as a hospital chaplain. The annual take-home salary hovered at $5000; I decided to forget the whole thing and took a job in development at Yale Divinity School. It was a cold, snowbound winter in New England with lots of time to think. By springtime I was on my way back home, ready to do whatever it took to be ordained.

One year's hospital chaplaincy and a set of ordination exams later, I was ordained a deacon in June of 1983. It was like marrying after a ten-year engagement; my hands did not even sweat. The chronology fades after that. I was ordained priest eleven months later on the feast day of Saint Julian of Norwich, and am in my second year at All Saints' Church, Atlanta. My title is "Assistant Rector and Coordinator of Youth and Adult Education," but what that boils down to is a little bit of everything: counseling street people, officiating at marriages, renting a truck for the youth hayride, leading the Thursday morning Bible study. I am easily overwhelmed by it all, but have not regretted my choice.

Preaching is what I enjoy most, and do best. Not only because I love the work of communication, of creating images and choosing words, but also because preaching is how I pray. The process of picking a text, wrestling with it, losing myself in it, finally hearing what it has to say and finding some new way to pass that word on to my congregation — that process is my most reliable experience of God, and I remain in awe of it.

People regularly ask me what is next, what I want to be doing five years from now, and the answer escapes me. I could not have predicted today; how can I foresee tomorrow? What I know is that this vocation challenges me to think more about *how* I will be a priest instead of *where* I will be or doing *what*. Meanwhile, my work teaches me what I need to know, and there is no end in sight.

PENTECOST II
Jeremiah 20:7-13
Matthew 10:16-33

June 24, 1984
All Saints' Church
Atlanta, Georgia

The sermons that follow were all written during my first year as a priest. I was not new to the pulpit; I had been preaching as a layperson for several years, but never on such a regular basis, nor to such a responsive congregation. All Saints' is an urban parish of 1100 souls, most of whom earn their livings as professionals. They are an educated lot, who are not afraid to question their faith or to put it to work in urban ministries. My hope, whenever I preach, is to give them a new perspective on the gospel, a new experience of it that both feeds and challenges them.

Part of my own discipline in preaching is to stick to the lectionary, and usually to pick the most troublesome lection as my text. In the sermon that follows, that text is from Matthew's gospel: "Behold, I send you out as a sheep in the midst of wolves." The text makes it clear that believers will suffer in this world; my curiosity had to do with how sophisticated, upper-class Episcopalians live with this truth, especially when it comes to witnessing to their faith.

As far as the church is concerned, today is the second Sunday of Pentecost, but after listening to this morning's lessons we might wonder whether something like "Persecution Sunday" might be more appropriate. For there is simply no mistaking today's theme: to bear the word of God into the world means to suffer. Jeremiah, the psalmist, and Jesus through his apostle Matthew all raise the same chorus: if you're going to be a disciple you'd better wear your running shoes, because the fur is going to fly.

And that was no prophecy but actual fact for them. Jeremiah's sad speech comes the morning after his humiliation at the hands of Pashur, the chief priest in the temple in Jerusalem, who beat him and put him in stocks overnight for preaching in the streets. Jeremiah is understandably crushed. He is only doing what almighty God CHOSE him to do, and while he may not expect to become a celebrity for it, he at least expects that people will LISTEN to him, that the God who sent him will also open the ears of those to whom he has been sent.

But that turns out not to be the case. No one praises Jeremiah for his wisdom, or thanks him for his warning, or respects him as a messenger of God. They jeer at him, and throw rocks at him, and altogether reject him. It hurts his feelings, and with alarming honesty he complains bitterly to God: "O Lord, thou hast deceived me and I was deceived; thou art stronger than I, and thou hast prevailed." A more accurate translation is even sadder still, because the Hebrew word for "deceived" more often means "seduced," which means that Jeremiah is accusing God of taking advantage of him, of promising more than he delivers: of promising love and good feelings and bowers of roses, promising happily-ever-after when all he really had in mind was using Jeremiah, using him and then casting him off on a cruel people who would make mean fun of his gullibility.

And like a lover scorned he vows not to be used again: "I will not mention him," the prophet says of Yahweh, "or speak any more in his name." But the love remains, and grows, and finally erupts, forcing Jeremiah to admit: "There is in my heart as it were a burning fire shut up in my bones, and I am weary of holding it in, and I cannot."

The prophet learns, in other words, that his consuming love affair with God has nothing to do with comfort and everything to do with pain, but he also learns that the pain of going on, of continuing to love and serve a fiery God is NOTH-ING compared to the pain of stopping and letting the fire go out.

So that's the word from the Old Testament. Skip six or seven hundred years and note that Matthew says more or less the same thing: "Behold, I send you out as sheep in the midst of wolves," Jesus says to his disciples. "You will be hated by all for my name's sake." "When they persecute you in one town, flee to the next." It is not a particularly attractive proposition, not a job we would go out of our way to get, but there it is again: to bear the word of God into the world means to suffer.

It was true then, and there are many parts of the world where it is true now: in Iran, behind the Iron Curtain, in El Salvador: places where missionaries are tortured and nuns are shot dead, where teaching people to read and telling them about their birthright as free children of God are considered revolutionary acts. Jeremiah and Matthew would be at home in such places; Jesus is certainly at home in them, reminding his disciples now as then that the word of God is not bedtime reading but dynamite, designed to blow the powers of darkness off the face of the earth, and that those who carry it risk their very lives to do so.

But what about us? What about here and now, in these United States, in this great city of Atlanta, where the church is not a persecuted minority but a respectable community of relatively comfortable believers? What do we know about dying for our faith? Who among us has been arrested for praying in public or flogged at Peachtree Center for confessing Christ as Lord? Not that we should ever wish for it to be so, but the best way to learn from today's lessons is to try to see ourselves clearly in their light.

Our world is different, radically different. We suffer — let there be no mistake about that — but we suffer so differently, under such different circumstances — more on the inside than on the outside. Our persecutions, such as they are, are much more subtle than Jeremiah's or those of the early disciples. Few of us fulfill our ministry by evangelizing on streetcorners or preaching from town to town.

Many more of us are called to witness in our homes, in our neighborhoods, at our jobs, often among people who already call themselves Christians.

At a cocktail party, for instance. You're standing around with a glass in your hand, enjoying a perfectly benign conversation when someone tells a cruel joke or makes a pointed remark. The God in you bristles, and your face gets hot. A dozen possible responses run through your mind, which you eliminate one by one: too rude, too judgmental, too self-righteous, too pushy. You note out loud that your glass is empty and excuse yourself to return to the bar, wondering why you come to these things, anyway. Later, at home, you replay the scene and construct a perfect response, but it's useless now. A knot of self-loathing roots in your stomach and keeps you awake.

Or maybe you're at work, opening the file on a new project. You've done well at your job and have been rewarded with greater responsibility, but the more you read the worse you feel. There's something wrong here, something crooked going on, and you're being asked to participate in it. You confide in a colleague, who assures you that it's done all the time and that no one is really hurt by it. Your friend furthermore reminds you that to rock the boat could cost you your job and that you have bills to pay, children to send to college. You weigh the odds and decide to keep your objections to yourself. It continues to nag at you, but you don't want to cause trouble. And the knot in your stomach grows.

Name your own scenario: there's no end to the variations on this theme. If Jeremiah's complaint is that he cannot contain the fire in his bones, ours is that we cannot seem to let it out. The word of God smolders inside us, threatening to turn everything to ash, and our fear of keeping it locked up is exceeded only by our fear of letting it out. All HELL might break loose! We might lose our friends, our jobs, our wits! Surely THAT'S not what the church is about — it's about being nice to people, isn't it, and avoiding conflict, and providing comfort? Isn't it?

Now I am not about to stand up here and exhort us all to become modern day Jeremiahs. Only God can make a prophet, but what this prophet in particular and the Messiah who came after him, what they want to relieve us of is our inordinate fear of suffering. What they want to show us is that God is not found at a safe distance from grief and hurt but smack through the middle of it. And that goes against every sensible cell in our bodies, each one of which is dedicated to self-preservation. It also goes against our popular understanding of the church, which is likewise concerned with its own survival.

If you need proof, just check out the churches that are not only surviving but thriving — what do they promise? A clear vision of what is good in the world and what is evil, with sure protection from what is evil; a warm, close relationship with God; deliverance from illness and hardship; the answer to prayer and — occasionally — material riches as God's return for true faith. In a word: they promise comfort and security, the sort of happily-ever-after that Jeremiah wanted so desperately from his beloved God and did not get.

Even in our own, more subtly Episcopal way, we pursue some of that same standard. We do all that we do here in order to show those outside the church that faith *works*, that it makes us relatively happy, peaceful people – good citizens, social exemplars, people who carry more than our own load. And we'd be crazy to do otherwise – how many new members would we attract if we billed this not as a place to gain something but a place to lose everything, to be set on fire and helped to suffer? It simply would not sell. But where do we – where does any Christian who prays for protection from suffering – get the idea that we deserve more and better than Jesus got?

Scott Peck's book *The Road Less Traveled* has been on the best-seller list for some time now. I've just gotten around to reading it and can understand why. The first line is a grabber all by itself: "Life is difficult," it says. But most of us, Peck goes on to say, don't fully accept this simple truth. Most of us, like Jeremiah, complain bitterly about our problems, our suffering, as if life were on the whole easy, as if it *should* be easy. And because life is difficult, most of us embark pretty early on a mission to make our lives as pain-free as possible, to skirt the suffering that threatens us from every side and pour water on as many fires as possible.

For some of us that means making lots of money, for others it means avoiding relationships, for others it means seeking a happily-ever-after relationship with God. Whatever it means, the end result is always to insulate ourselves from suffering, to pad ourselves so well that even if we fall we won't get hurt.

And that is how the fear of suffering comes to dominate our lives. It is all futile, of course. The suffering creeps in anyway, and it doesn't take long to learn that our insulation keeps us away from as much joy as pain, but the most treacherous effect of our padding is that we cease to grow inside it. The more successful we are at living pain-free lives, the more shallow and hollow those lives become, until there is very little life left in them at all. But the fear keeps its grip, by convincing us that our survival depends on avoiding suffering. It tells us, with tremendous authority, that if we do not protect ourselves we will die.

To all of this today's Gospel speaks very, very clearly. "Have no fear," "Do not fear," "Fear not," Jesus says to his disciples. It's fear that will do you in, not suffering. No pain on earth can harm you as much as the paralysis of fear, which is a creeping deadness of the soul, which is the one thing you *should* fear. But if it's life you want, forsake comfort and follow me, through suffering and even death into more life than you are able to imagine.

This is the great mystery of the faith, the mystery that makes the church in any time or place a radical presence on earth. In the middle of a world bent with fear of suffering and seeking security on every side, the church holds up a different standard, repeating the simple truth that suffering is not the enemy, but deadness of soul, and that the best security is surrender to all the joy and pain that life has to bring.

In a society dedicated to the pursuit of pleasure, the church turns secular values upside down. If something hurts, the culture says, get rid of it: hard job, painful relationships, prickly conversations — if they hurt, dump them, and move on to something more comfortable. On the contrary, the church says, if something hurts, stick with it, work through it, because that's how your soul grows – not through the easy passages but through the hardest and most painful ones.

It is a hard, hard lesson we are given to struggle with this morning. No one wants to suffer, and certainly it is not divine will that we suffer, but when the hot word of God is poured over a cold, cold world, THINGS BREAK, and it is into that brokenness that we are called, into whatever big or small piece we find in front of us, with fire in our bones, to show a frightened world that it is not the heat of the fire that we fear, but the chill that lies ahead if the fire goes out. Amen.

PENTECOST X
Isaiah 56:1-7
Romans 11:13-15, 29-32
Matthew 15:21-28

August 19, 1984
All Saints' Church
Atlanta, Georgia

The two most important influences on my preaching have been Fred Craddock and Frederick Buechner, both of whom I heard deliver the annual Beecher Lectures in preaching at Yale. When Craddock came to teach at Emory in 1979, I was privileged to hear him often and in the flesh; my acquaintance with Buechner has been limited to reading every word the man has written. What both of these preachers teach me is the power of images.

People change when their dominant images — of themselves, of the world, of God — change. My task as a preacher, then, is to give my listeners vivid images from which to choose. Everything I do in sermon preparation has to do with this task. Whether I am translating Hebrew, reading commentaries, or just free-associating on a text, what I am doing is waiting for The Image to emerge, the one that will give my listeners a new choice. In this sermon, the image I sought to replace was that of the limited self, the part of all of us that wants to shout, "Enough! I cannot do any more!" Jesus himself provided the alternative.

Today is one of those days a preacher is tempted to preach on the psalm, or some theme unrelated to the lessons, or better yet, to invite a traveling mime troupe to perform in place of the sermon: anything to avoid trying to make sense of the Gospel, which shows our gentle Jesus in a mighty peculiar light.

And not only peculiar, but downright rude, if the truth be told. First he refuses to answer a woman pleading for his help, then denies that he has anything to offer "her kind," and finally likens her to a dog before the sheer force of her faith changes something in him and he decides to fulfill her request after all.

Now granted, she's a Canaanite, one of the really vile Gentiles whom the Jews regarded as outcasts, as lost causes. Not three pages earlier, Jesus himself has warned his disciples to steer clear of them, and to devote all their energies to the lost sheep of Israel. The only catch is that the lost sheep don't seem to want to be found — in spite of his undivided attention to them, his own people, they are not rushing to respond to his shepherd's call.

In today's story he has just come from Nazareth, his own hometown, where his friends and family have doubted his authority and taken offense at his teaching.

-125-

He has recently received word from Jerusalem that John the Baptist has lost his head to a dancing girl, and he has tried at this blow to withdraw from the crowds for a while, but the crowds have followed him and he has, with five loaves and two fishes, fed them all. Then there was the storm at sea and Peter's wish to cross the water, foiled by the disciple's fear and doubt. Everywhere Jesus turns he finds need, need and people who want what he can do for them but are blind to who he is. He is at the frayed end of his rope, and all but used up.

Then comes this Canaanite woman crying out to him to heal her daughter. He tells her plainly that he has nothing to offer her, but she persists, calling him by NAME: O Lord, Son of David. It is the title his own people have denied him, spoken now by one of the pagans he has been taught to avoid all his life. It must have seemed a mean trick of fate to him, to hear what he most wanted to hear coming from the mouth of someone he least wanted to hear it from.

But what makes this story so unusual — and so touching — is that in it we witness a crucial change in Jesus' own understanding of who he is and what he has been called to do. During his verbal duel with this foreign woman, something in him snaps and his horizons expand. He is no longer a Messiah called only to the lost sheep of Israel, but God's chosen redeemer of the whole world, Jews and Gentiles both, beginning with this Canaanite woman.

Through her faith he learns that God's purpose for him is bigger than he had imagined, that there IS enough of him to go around, and in that moment there is no going back to the limits he observed even a moment ago. The old boundaries won't contain this new vision — he must rub them out and draw them bigger, to include this foreign woman today and who knows what tomorrow. It looks like answering God's call means that he can no longer control his ministry or narrow his mission; there is no more safety or certainty for him, no more guarding against loss or hanging on to cherished notions of the way things ought to be. Faith works like a lever on him, opening his arms wider and wider until there is room for the whole world, until he allows them to be NAILED open on the cross.

It is the same story throughout all of this morning's lessons, over and over. God's call involves outgrowing old boundaries, embracing the outcast, and giving up the notion that there is any such thing as a lost cause.

In Isaiah's time, it was not Canaanites but eunuchs and foreigners who were believed to be outside God's mercy. Neither group had much choice in the matter. Foreigners were often present in Israel because they had been brought there in chains; and even if they had come freely in search of a better life and confessed Yahweh as Lord, they were barred from public worship of him simply on the grounds of race (their blood wasn't Jewish), and even their animals were forbidden for sacrificial use.

But at least they had children. The eunuchs had no such comfort. Although they often held high offices in government or household service, they too were barred from worship, as were all impaired and defective persons. Their grief was double, then — not only were they excluded from the community of the covenant, but since they had no heirs to carry on their names, they faced personal extinction as well.

Lost causes, both of them, not worth bothering with, but Isaiah's surprising prophecy is that things are not as they seem, that Yahweh does not hold the same prejudices as his people, and that faithful eunuchs and foreigners will outrank the unfaithful of Israel when the kingdom comes.

Finally, in Paul's letter to the Romans, we pick up in the middle of the endless squabble between the Jews and the Gentiles. In short, Paul warns the Gentile Christians not to gloat because they have seen the light where the Jews have not. "For the gifts and the call of God are irrevocable," he says, meaning that whether the Jews are willing or not, God won't give up on them, will never put them on the shelf as a lost cause. It may look for all the world like they're missing the boat, but things are not as they seem, and the only absolute certainty is that God's arms always open wider than ours know how.

So. Canaanites, eunuchs, foreigners, Gentiles, Jews — ancient fables all, but what do they have to do with us? There is the obvious interpretation, of course — that we are surrounded by similar outcasts, equally lost causes, and that God calls us to expand our boundaries to include them, and to include the possibility that they may reach God's holy mountain ahead of us.

Like sheltering the homeless, for instance, when we can only shelter a few out of the thousands who walk the streets, when one night's shelter does nothing to change the squalor of their lives, when we know the poor will be with us always.

Or like caring for the dying and disabled, when resources are scarce for the LIVING, when there will be no tangible return on our investment, when we know we cannot beat death.

Or like staying open to people who are different from us, when they challenge our values, when we need desperately to put SOMEONE down so that we can feel better about ourselves, when it is downright exhausting to entertain every stranger as a child of God.

Fill in the blanks: Who are your lost causes? Who are outside the fold, dry trees, foreigners, apostates, dogs? List them, and then look again, for the face of God where you least expect it, and least want it to be.

But that's the obvious interpretation, like saying that the moral of this morning's gospel lesson is that we should all love Canaanites. That's nice and clear, but the more subtle interpretation is harder to define. Its focus is not on the woman at all but on Jesus himself, and the momentous shift that occurs in his self-understanding. He grows before our very eyes. Answering God's irrevocable call tugs him further than he meant to go, and he discovers that his old intentions are no longer big enough, that God has something far bigger in store for him.

In terms of lost causes, this shift has less to do with lost causes OUTSIDE of us than those that live INSIDE of us — the parts of ourselves we regard as beyond hope, beyond change. For Jesus it was the part of himself that said he was not called to the Gentiles, that he had nothing to offer them. That was where he drew the line, but the irrevocable call of God tugged him over it, and there was no going back.

For us, it may be the part of ourselves that says we cannot really get close to anyone, that the old scars are too painful; or the part of us that says we can never measure up to what people expect of us, or the part that says we cannot ever have what we really want, that life is full of disappointments and we had better just get used to it. Whatever the nuance, it is the part of ourselves that says we cannot change, that the narrow boundaries we have drawn for ourselves are safe and that our occasional visions of something more and better are unrealistic, or dangerous, but in any case impossible.

That kind of self-limitation is what today's gospel challenges, and challenges fiercely. The gifts and the call of God are irrevocable, and whenever we limit who we are and what we can do, that call wreaks havoc on those limitations. Whenever we draw a line and say we cannot go any further, that same call beckons us into new territory, where we may well formulate new limits and draw new lines, but none that last very long. That's the way it is when you've been called out by God — once he has called you out he never calls you to go back — whatever YOU choose to do — God never calls you to go back.

What that means day to day is noticing the difference between the times we are hanging back, clinging to our limits, and the times we are moving out, pushing into new and often frightening territory. It's a difference you can FEEL, the difference between withdrawing from people, failing to meet their eyes, keeping a tight rein on our feelings, protecting ourselves, keeping lists of our failures, rehearsing the reasons why we cannot change. It's the difference between that and putting ourselves in the path of strangers, being the first to extend our hands, aching with empathy for a world in travail, trying new things, changing our minds.

It's a painful difference, to be sure. As painful as it was for Jesus to hear an outcast call him Lord when his own people would not; as painful as it was for him to step beyond generations of prejudice and respond to her faith; as painful as it is for any one of us to let go of whatever piece of wreckage has been keeping us afloat and launch out on the formidable swim to shore.

Let go! Step out! Tip your hat to a Canaanite, invite a eunuch to lunch, order octopus for dinner, learn to square dance, ask that street person what his life is like, stop smoking, lose weight, mend that broken friendship, call home, make that career change, write that difficult letter, take that risk, renounce playing it safe! You've got nothing to lose but your life the way it has been, and there's lots more life where that came from.

That, as best I can say it, is the subtler message in today's lessons. With Jesus as our model — and our saviour — we are called, irrevocably, to step over the lines we have drawn for ourselves, to do battle with everything that says we and those around us cannot change, and to step out into the unlimited, abundant life that God has been holding out to us since the world began. Amen.

PENTECOST XVIII
Isaiah 25:1-9
Philippians 4:4-13
Matthew 22:1-14

October 14, 1984
All Saints' Church, Atlanta, Georgia

*A parishioner recently reminded me that many of my sermons begin with apologies or dis-
claimers, usually about the hardness of the text at hand. Since I am the one who searches
out the hard passage, my complaint is usually rhetorical — a way of letting my listeners
know how I feel about my text — but there are Sundays when I worry that the gospel con-
tains no Good News at all.*

*This sermon was prepared for one of those Sundays, when Matthew's gospel was full of
reproach and condemnation. I researched the passage obsessively, hoping for some nuance
in the Greek, some previously undiscovered explanation for its venom. What I got — less
by studying the passage than by living through it — was an image, of what it must be like to
give up fear and deception in favor of self-revelation. Writing the sermon became a spiritual exercise, a prayer, a case-in-point of why preaching is at once the most difficult and
valuable thing I do. There is no end to the Good News.*

As many of you know, the church staff gathers every Tuesday afternoon
to plan, to pray, and to discuss the lessons assigned for the next Sunday. The
preacher of the week presides over this discussion and hopes for a good head
start on a sermon.

When I heard the lesson from Paul's letter to the Philippians I was overjoyed —
finally, a chance to preach about rejoicing, about truth, honor, justice, purity,
loveliness — all those positive, compelling virtues. Then I heard the lesson
from the gospel according to Matthew and sobered right up — it is a parable of
murder and rejection, with an ending that makes no sense at all. Why should
someone recruited off the street to come to a wedding just happen to be wearing
a wedding garment? And why should he be cast into outer darkness because he
is not? Clearly, this is the lesson we must wrestle with this morning, as tempting
as it is to ignore it as a piece of ancient mumbo-jumbo.

What it is, according to the commentaries, is an ancient allegory about God's
involvement, first with the Jews and then with the Gentiles — all of whom have
been invited to feast at God's table when Christ comes again, but few of whom
will choose to come, and fewer still who will be chosen to stay once they get
there.

Jesus tells the story during what we may imagine to be the worst — and what we KNOW to be the last — week of his life. He has ridden into Jerusalem on a donkey amidst great excitement and has headed straight to the temple, where he has overturned tables and driven out all the peddlers and shoppers. It's not like him, right? But watch — this last week is full of strange, angry events.

The next morning, headed back to the temple for round two, Jesus stops along the way to pluck fruit from a fig tree. But the tree is barren — probably because it is still springtime and not yet the SEASON for the tree to bear fruit. But nonetheless Jesus curses the tree and it dies. Again, it's not like him. But neither is this week like any other. Time is closing in on him, speeding to an end, and nothing seems to have changed. There is corruption in the temple, and no fruit on the tree, and disbelief everywhere, even among those closest to him. Has he failed? Will he go to his death without accomplishing that for which he was sent? He must try harder, do more, seek his opponents out and win them over before time runs out. This urgency changes his tone, sharpens his tongue until there is no middle ground left. Choose, he says to everyone within hearing, choose whom you will serve before it is too late, or else be cast into outer darkness.

It is during this week, with this urgency, that he returns to the temple and confronts the chief priests and elders. He tells them three stories in a row, three stories which we, too, have heard in a row these last three Sundays. All of them, in their different ways, wind up with the same warning. The Jews have been invited to share in God's sonship, in God's harvest, in his son's wedding feast, but have rejected the invitation and will be rejected by God in return.

Today's story is the third such warning and the most eloquent. If we iron out the allegory, it goes like this: At the end of all time a king, Yahweh, gives a wedding feast for his son Jesus, who is marrying humankind. Yahweh sends his servants, his prophets, and apostles to call those who have been invited to the feast — to Israel, that is, God's chosen people — but they refuse for various reasons and they even martyr his messengers. So God declares them unworthy, destroys them, and sends his servants to gather a new crowd — Gentiles this time — and they come; but they are a motley crew. To show everyone that being invited late to the heavenly banquet is no excuse for coming unprepared, the king tosses out one badly dressed Gentile as an example to the rest that God's standards will not be lowered just because his chosen people did not come.

Now you know why we like to leave parables alone — this one has begun to sound more like one of Aesop's fables than the word of God. To confuse our interpretation even more, scholars tell us that there are really two stories here collapsed into one, and that we don't even know the original beginning of the wedding garment story. The guest probably had time to go home and change his clothes but didn't. He was probably not treated as unreasonably as the present story makes it sound.

But that route is tedious and endless. However we GOT the parable, we've got it and it is frightening. Frightening because we can imagine it so well; we know how it FEELS. We have all arrived somewhere or another in the nick of time, breathless, worrying that we left the iron on at home or forgot to lock the door. But we make it and hope we'll know how to act, what to say. It looks like a great party — tables heaped with food and a crowd of musicians warming up over in the corner. And here comes the king — HELP! Do you curtsey or bow? Speak first or wait to be spoken to? But he doesn't wait for you to figure it out — he walks right up to you — you put on your most humble, endearing face as he grips your shoulder and says, "Friend." At first you're flattered — FRIEND — hey, the king LIKES you. But something about the glint in his eye, the weight of his hand on your shoulder suddenly makes your stomach sink like a stone. All at once you know you're in trouble and it's like a bad dream or an Alfred Hitchcock movie. Everything that seemed wonderful just a moment ago has become deadly; all the colors have melted and run together in a muddy brown, and you're in deep, deep trouble, without a clue about what you've done wrong.

"How did you get in here without a wedding garment?" the king asks you, and it occurs to you that perhaps you are naked — oh no, not another one of those dreams — you have no earthly idea WHAT you are wearing, but you cannot take your eyes from his to look. You cannot move your mouth either, not even to say you're sorry; but before you can clear your throat, you have been bound hand and foot and thrown out the door into the starless night, utterly, utterly rejected.

Now to tell you the story from that perspective is to make a confession — that I see more of myself in the badly dressed guest than in the other characters. Why not identify with the king's servants or with one of the GOOD guests? Original sin, maybe. But when I hear, "For many are called, but few are chosen," I get nervous. I begin to do intensive research on what it takes to get chosen. I review my wardrobe, check the oil in my lamp, take a No-Doz. When the wedding banquet begins, I want a seat.

It's not a matter of receiving an invitation, see, because EVERYONE has been invited: the Jews and the Gentiles, the chief priests and the barefooted disciples, the elders of the community along with the harlots and the tax collectors. We ALL have been invited, from Tuxedo Road and the Union Mission, from the Cathedral of Saint Philip and the Krishna commune on Ponce de Leon, homemakers and streetwalkers, IRS executives and X-rated bookstore owners — ALL have been called to God's table. But what today's gospel says is that few of us will be chosen to sit down and eat at the end of time.

So what does it take to be chosen? Details. I want details. To stay within the parameters of today's story, it first of all takes choosing to come to the banquet in the first place. The whole first batch of invitations went out to people who chose other things to do. They were too busy to come to the feast, had other more pressing matters to attend to – a board meeting to prepare for, a prospective client to call on, a vacation planned since March. They treated the king's banquet, the invitation to his holy table, like any other social engagement and were taken off heaven's guest list for good.

So the first thing it takes to be chosen is to choose to respond to the invitation, to say yes to coming into the king's presence, as risky a proposition as that may be — because to come into his presence is to consent to be seen, and known, and judged, to be chosen or cast into the outer darkness. So how do we prepare for that? Does it really have to do with something as superficial as what we have on? Next thing you know the king will be checking under our fingernails. I mean, all that really matters is how we feel inside, right? The inner disposition of our hearts — it's not how we look or act or even what we say, but what we believe deep down inside that counts, right?

Wrong. According to today's piece of the gospel, we are called to look on the outside like we are on the inside, to be so genuinely who and what we are that there is no division between our insides and our outsides, no blockade between what we believe and the way we live. That is what we need to sit at the king's wedding feast, and if our outsides do not yet match our insides, if we have said yes to the wedding feast but have failed to reflect that yes in how we live and move and have our being, then we're not yet ready to sit down.

In grammar, in geometry, in theology, even, the word is CONGRUITY: the state or quality of agreement, in which the parts of a whole are in harmony. To have congruity in our lives is to let our grain show, without veneer, to be of a solid piece. When people look at us, what they see is what they get.

Congruity may be easier to define by its absence. We have all known INCONGRUOUS people — whose nice behavior is beyond reproach but whose anger rolls off them in waves; or people who pledge you their loyal support but tell you they have a party to go to the night your world collapses; or any number of people whose impeccable lives you envy until you receive the news of addiction, divorce, depression. Whatever the particular details, you know the signs: the unsettling distance between what people are telling you about themselves and what their lives are showing you; a hollowness, an echo almost, as if when you tapped on their surfaces it would take a very long time for their souls to find the door.

If we are unusually perceptive, we may even be able to read signs in ourselves: the distance between who we want to be and who we are, between how we present ourselves to others and who we know ourselves to be.

In its own convoluted, antiquated way, that's what this morning's gospel challenges. It challenges us to root out the incongruities in our lives, to come out of our hiding places even if that means owning up to some pretty unsavory truths about ourselves, and to close the distance between who we are and the way we present ourselves to others, including God. For some of us that may mean opening up to the hurt child inside us who has been coming across as an angry adult;

or lifting our cool, self-controlled lids and letting a lot of unruly feelings spill out; or giving up our copyrighted aloofness and admitting how we long, ache, YEARN to be loved. Whatever our particular dramas have been, whatever we have worn up to this point, what we are called to now is to dress for the banquet, a magnificent, holy, end-of-all-time meal.

And you don't need me to tell you how to dress for a special occasion. First you find a place to CHANGE, some place with lots of light and a mirror to see yourself in and everything you own there from which to choose. Then you strip — you become naked, and if you haven't already bathed you take the time now to come clean, to wash yourself from head to foot and let all the dirt go down the drain. Then it's back to the mirror, choosing what you will put on with care, checking each garment as you go for appropriateness and beauty. You choose what fits best, what fits you and fits the occasion.

But here's where dressing for this particular banquet is different from all the other grand occasions of our lives, because we're not looking for the flattering fit this time, the one that conceals our faults, but for the revealing one, the one that shows us as we are. And if we do not wear that one, the king will know that we have not worn our wedding garment, and will send us out into the darkness where people weep and gnash their teeth.

At least that's what the reading this morning says. Another way of saying the same thing is that until we're dressed for the feast, we have no business inside anyway; and once we ARE dressed nothing can keep us out. It's less a matter of being rewarded or punished by the king than it is a matter of being recognized by him for who and what we are. His choices at the wedding feast will in all likelihood mirror the choices we have been making all the way there.

God knows it's a lifelong process, getting dressed for that feast, learning to see ourselves clearly enough to know what to put on, to look on the outside like who we are on the inside, to be who we are called to be. And thank God we have been given a foretaste of that banquet in the Holy Eucharist, which is the meal where we are all learning about wholeness, about congruity, about getting our proverbial acts together. Every time we prepare ourselves for this meal, inside and out — every time we clothe and present ourselves at this table for the food and drink we need, we get another chance to try something different, to take a new risk, to let a little more of ourselves show.

We have been called, and we are here. The wedding banquet is yet to come, but, God willing, we'll be there too. As for whether or not we'll be chosen to stay and sit down, we don't seem to have any guarantees. What we do have is the gift of a holy meal, and faith in the bridegroom who shares it with us, and time enough left to ponder these things. Amen.

VITAE
Janice M. Bracken

Born: *Richmond, VA, May 17, 1957*
Siblings: *Older Brother*
Religious Background: *Episcopal*
Marital Status: *Single*

Parents:	Mother	Father
Born	*1922*	*1925*
Education	*High School*	*High School*
Occupation	*Homemaker*	*Private Contractor, Retired*
Religious Background	*Episcopal*	*Episcopal*

Education: *St. Catherine's School, Richmond, VA, 1975*
University of Virginia, B.A. with highest distinction, Religious Studies, 1978
Candler School of Theology, M. Div. summa cum laude, 1981
(Academic Excellence Award)

Ordination: *Deacon, July 18, 1981*
Priest, June 26, 1982

Seminary:
Why?

Many years of lay ministry; mentor in college was Jesuit priest; decided to try seminary to choose among work in hospital, school, or parish setting

Reactions to seminary decision — Some people surprised; most pre-seminary friends not affected in any negative sense.

Sources of support — Home parish, vestry, faculty.

Roadblocks — None in seminary.

Significant events — An inter-seminary award, the Jordan, Israel, Greece Adventure, a study/travel trip to the Middle East.

Reflections – Pastoral care classes were a good experience; "how to's" of running a parish would be a good curriculum addition, also development of effective ministries to youth and young adults. In general, see ordained women as adding a balance to ministry; opening up new dimensions in pastoral care, counseling, and sacramental ministry.

Career: *Assistant rector, St. Peter's, Rome, Georgia, 1983-present.*
Future goals — Multi-clergy staff a priority for now.

Relationship with other clergywomen: *Feel very close to other clergywomen.*

Sources invigorating ministry: *Diversity of parish ministry, teaching adult education, preaching.*

Theological Interests: *Liturgical theology, pastoral care, Bible study.*

Reaction to preaching: *Marvelous; parishioners comment on the sermons and discuss them.*

Suggestions for those considering the ministry: *Be realistic about employment, what you sacrifice, the newness of women in orders, and your own call to ministry. Claim your talents, exercise your gifts, expect many challenges, and be open to the joy.*

Activities/Interests: *Traveling (hope for Italy this summer), collect Coca-Cola memorabilia, dinner with friends, needlework.*

VITAE

Eloise Hally

Born: *Boston, MA, May 28, 1943*
Siblings: *Older sister, younger brother*
Religious Background: *Congregational, Roman Catholic*
Marital Status: *Divorced*
Children: *Claire Hally Smith (9)*

Parents:	Mother	Father
Born	*1910*	*1916*
Education	*Cornell University, B.S.*	*High School, Cont. Ed.*
Occupation	*Housewife, dietitian*	*Career Navy, gov't Civil Servant*
Religious Background	*Congregational*	*Roman Catholic*

Education:	*Paris American High 1957-59 North Quincy High, MA, 1960* *Vassar College, A.B., Economics, 1964* *Duke University, Ph.D. Candidate, Economics, 1973* *Candler School of Theology, M. Div., magna cum laude, 1982 (Preaching Award)*
Ordination:	*Deacon, June 12, 1982; Priest, May 4, 1983, the Feast of St. Monica*
Other Careers:	*Peace Corps, Turkey, 1964-66* *Computer Programmer/Research Assistant* *Budget Examiner, U.S. Bureau of the Budget* *Visiting Assistant Professor of Economics, Emory University 1975-78*
Seminary: Why?	*Wanted the stuff of Sunday school at a deeper level; at first a personal quest for theology for issues of my own soul; then, for education for ministry.* *Reactions to seminary decision — Friends were excited and supportive.* *Sources of support — St. Luke's Church, Atlanta, Georgia; pastoral counselor; friends; other women in seminary and ministry.* *Significant events — Diocesan Experiment in Ministry; clinical quarter at Grady Hospital; parish internship; my own process in therapy.* *Reflections — Faculty important, had interest beyond the academic; focus on significance for Christian life in world and church; persistent quest for meaning.*
Career:	*Chaplain, Georgia Baptist Hospital (Clinical Pastoral Education) and pastoral counselor, 1984-present.* *Deacon and Assistant to the Rector, Church of the Atonement, Sandy Springs, Georgia, 1982-1983.* *Future goals — Rector, Assistant to Rector, especially Assistant for pastoral care, adult education; or run a pastoral counseling center at a church.*

Relationship with other clergywomen: *Among my closest friends; have participated in a multi-denominational clergywomen's support group; helpful to share with colleagues.*

Sources invigorating ministry: *Worship and prayer; parish life; therapy; clinical experience; biblical studies and sermon preparation.*

Theological Interests: *Bible and literary criticism; hermeneutics; theological reflection on clinical experience, Charles Gerkin's* The Living Human Document.

Suggestions for those considering ministry: *Be aware of the realities of getting a position once out of seminary, and of the difficulties of being a working mother.*

Activities/Interests: *Doing things with Claire, getting together with friends, movies, swimming.*

VITAE

E. Claiborne Jones

Born: *Durham, NC, Nov. 22, 1950*
Siblings: *Two older sisters*
Religious Background: *Episcopal*
Marital Status: *Single*

Parents:	Mother	Father
Born	*1911*	*1914*
Education	*Randolph-Macon Women's College, B.A.*	*Hampden-Sydney, B.A. University of Virginia, B.A., M.A., Ph.D.*
Occupation	*Reference Librarian, Housewife*	*Professor of Zoology; Vice Chancellor for Business and Finance, University of North Carolina*
Religious Background	*Episcopal, Methodist*	*Presbyterian, Episcopal*

Education:	*St. Margaret's School, Tappahannock, VA, 1968* *Mt. Holyoke College, 1968-69* *University of North Carolina, B.A., 1972, Religion and English* *Candler School of Theology, M. Div. cum laude, 1978 (Senior Preaching Award)*
Ordination:	*Deacon, June 10, 1978; Priest, June 12, 1979*
Other Careers:	*Secretary at Georgia Association for Pastoral Care.*
Seminary: Why?	*To make sense of life and my life; thought about seminary while in college but decided to wait before entering.* *Reactions to seminary decision — Concept of "why don't you marry a minister?" was present; support from laywomen's group; Candler faculty were very vocal in their support.* *Sources of support — Two other Episcopal women candidates.* *Roadblocks — Spent long time deciding whether to be ordained (am I willing to step into the unknown? how will I be received?).* *Significant events — Field work in urban church, crisis intervention center, and nursing home; learned much about what is really important in ministry; loved seminary.* *Reflections — Experiences in field work confirmed call to the ministry.*
Career:	*Holy Innocents', School Chaplain, 1979-present. Church of the Holy Spirit, Deacon, 1978-79.* *Future goals — Rector of small parish; director of non-profit organization.*

Relationship with other clergywomen: *Though the women differ, they are one another's bottom line support.*

Sources invigorating ministry: *Team teaching with colleagues; reading children's stories — the parable often gets to the point in a refreshing way.*

Theological Interests: *Preaching, liturgy, biblical studies.*

Reaction to preaching: *No longer any "active" sexism.*

Suggestions for those considering ministry: *Wait; don't expect it to solve personal problems; be unafraid.*

Activities/Interests: *Hiking, cooking and eating with friends, handwork, watercolors, reading novels, and time spent with 'family' of friends.*

VITAE

Camille S. Littleton

Born: *Anniston, AL, June 3, 1945*
Siblings: *Two younger sisters, one younger brother*
Religious Background: *Episcopal*
Marital Status: *married 1965-1976*
Children: *Allison (16)*

Parents:	Mother	Father
Born	*1922*	*1918*
Education	*Attended Brenau College*	*The Citadel*
Occupation	*Taught piano; created crossword puzzles for New York Times*	*Civil engineer; owns property development company.*
Religious Background	*Baptist, later Episcopal*	*Episcopal*

Education: *Anniston High School, Anniston, AL, 1963*
Auburn University, B.A., 1967, Journalism
Candler School of Theology, M. Div., 1978

Ordination: *Deacon, June 10, 1978; Priest, June 12, 1979*

Other Careers: *Journalist* — Columbus Ledger Enquirer, Athens Daily News, Marietta Daily Journal.

Seminary:
Why? *Returned to the church to give unity to intellectual questioning.*

Reactions to seminary decision — Why is she in seminary?

Sources of support — Another woman Episcopal candidate; close friends; family.

Roadblocks – At the time, women could not be ordained.

Significant events — Balancing single parenthood and school.

Reflections — Priority was and still is to family; being a good parent is part of being a good priest.

Career: *Associate Rector, St. James, Marietta, 1980-present.*

Future goals – Full-time parish priest; studies in math, physics, philosophy; studies in music.

Relationship with other clergywomen: *Provide support in addition to the rector; meet as a group several times a year; would like to do more.*

Sources invigorating ministry: *Fellow in Residence, University of the South, Sewanee, 1984; studying music in the liturgy; working with children singing; teaching confirmation class; parishioners.*

Theological Interests: *Inclusive theology; contemporary theologians, particularly women; music in liturgy; worship as a sustaining ritual.*

Reaction to preaching: *For the most part, very positive.*

Suggestions for those considering ministry: *Liturgy offers a great deal — realize there are flaws as well as good points in the church and its principles; recognize your personal life will be scrutinized.*

Activities/Interests: *Music (bought a piano first year out of seminary); Member of Royal School of Church Music; chanting class; voice and piano lessons.*

VITAE

Lori M. Lowe

Born: *Atlanta, GA, March 12, 1947*
Siblings: *Younger sister*
Religious Background: *Southern Baptist*
Marital Status: *Married 1966-83*
Children: *Melissa Diane Bishop (14), Stephen David Bishop, Jr. (12)
and Justin Lowe Bishop (9)*

Parents:	Mother	Father
Born	*1925*	*1923*
Education	*Georgia State University, B.A., 1972*	*Mercer University*
Occupation	*Bank, public relations, clerical work.*	*Career Navy; Ivan Allen Company*
Religious Background	*Methodist*	*Southern Baptist*

Education: *Avondale High School, Atlanta, GA
West Georgia College, 1965-66
Georgia State University, B.A., 1969, English
Candler School of Theology, M. Div., 1983*

Ordination: *Postulant for Holy Orders*

Other Careers: *Teacher, high school English*

Seminary:
Why?   *Wanted to be a missionary as a child, no role models for preacher, very active in church; began thinking of the ministry when a suburban housewife with young children.*

    Reactions to seminary decision — Others saw growth and change.

    Sources of support — Seminary community, other women in ministry.

    Roadblocks — Delays in formal process provide self-reflection.

    Significant events — Singing for Sam Young in the Candler Choraliers; primary responsibility for childcare; Member of Worship Committee, Social Justice Network, Candler Women's Caucus, Coordinating Council, Who's Who Among Students in American Colleges and Universities, St. Luke's internship.

    Reflections — Seminary intense growing period in life.

Career: *Present — Pastoral Assistant, St. Bartholomew's, Atlanta, Georgia.*

Future goals: *Associate rector and (eventually) rector; perhaps doctorate.*

Relationship with other clergywomen: *Very important; many personal and professional connections.*

Sources invigorating ministry: *Teaching teachers of the Bible; equipping laity in their ministry.*

Theological Interests: *Scriptures, teaching of laity; pastoral counseling.*

Reaction to preaching: *"You'll make a fine preacher some day;" moved more confidently into pastoral and preaching roles.*

Suggestions for those considering ministry: *The ministry for women requires incredible introspection.*

Activities/Interests: *Soprano with the Atlanta Bach Choir.*

VITAE

Doris Graf Smith

Born: *Atlanta, GA, July 24, 1946*
Siblings: *Older brother*
Religious Background: *Methodist*
Marital Status: *Married*
Children: *Margaret Kemper Smith (14), Archer Dickerson Smith, IV (9)*

Parents:	Mother	Father
Born	*1913*	*1905*
Education	*High School*	*Self-educated, supported younger siblings*
Occupation	*Executive secretary*	*Farmer*
Religious Background	*Episcopal*	*Methodist*

Education: *Therrell High School, Atlanta, GA, 1964*
University of Georgia, B.A., 1968, English, secondary education
Candler School of Theology, M. Div. Cum Laude, 1984

Ordination: *Deacon, June 1984*
Priest, May 1985

Other Careers: *Certified elementary school teacher, taught four years, freelance writing; consulting work, Interfaith, Inc.; one year of law school; state politics.*

Seminary:
Why? *Skills and desires were confined in ordained ministry.*

Reactions to seminary decision — Mother and husband's parents may have been skeptical at first, but were extremely supportive in a very practical sense (typing and childcare); husband was totally supportive and proud.

Sources of support — Parents, husband, children, and Diocese of Atlanta.

Roadblocks — Studying after being out of school so many years; juggling family responsibilities.

Significant events — Parish work gave opportunity to feel more a leader, less a student.

Reflections — Clinical Pastoral Education was invaluable, need more Christian Education work, for example, experience in curriculum design.

Career: *Deacon, St. Catherine's Church, Marietta, Georgia, 1984-present.*
Future goals — Rector; more writing; working on an Episcopal curriculum.

Relationship with other clergywomen: *Similar to relationships with male clergy — for advice, teaching, support. Thankful for those ahead of me; I am more accepted because others came before me.*

Sources invigorating ministry: *Cacophony of past experiences which are now being used.*

Theological Interests: *Stewardship of self; Presence of communion; Tillich's concepts integrated with pastoral care.*

Reaction to preaching: *Parishioners positive; sermons are getting a little easier to write; no longer feel pressure to hit a home run every time.*

Suggestions for those considering ministry: *Ask the questions — Which ministry? What form will your ministry take?*

Activities/Interests: *Family; interior decorating, reading, singing.*

VITAE
Barbara Brown Taylor

Born: *Lafayette, IN, Sept. 21, 1951*
Siblings: *Two younger sisters*
Religious Background: *Catholic, Methodist, Presbyterian, Episcopal*
Marital Status: *Married*

Parents:	Mother	Father
Born	*1928*	*1926*
Education	*University of Denver, B.A., 1949, Psychology*	*University of S. Dakota, B.A., University of Denver, M.A., Purdue University, Ph.D., Psychology*
Occupation	*Real Estate*	*Psychotherapist*
Religious Background	*Methodist, Episcopal*	*Roman Catholic, Episcopal*

Education: *Druid Hills High School, Decatur, GA, 1969*
Emory University, B.A. Cum Laude, 1973, Religion
Yale Divinity School, M. Div., 1976

Ordination: *Deacon, June 11, 1983*
Priest, May 8, 1984

Other Careers: *Assistant to the Dean, Candler School of Theology, 1976-81.*
Assistant Director of Development, Yale Divinity School, 1981-82.

Seminary:
Why? *Rockefeller Trial Year in Seminary Award (all expenses paid for one year).*

Reactions to seminary decision — Had not decided on ordained ministry at the time.

Sources of support — Episcopal community at Yale; Rowan Greer, professor of New Testament; David Boulton, rector of Christ Church, New Haven.

Roadblocks — None at semimary; best experience of community and friends.

Significant events — Reformation Day, participating in service with Henri Nouwen (Roman Catholic) and George Lindbeck (Lutheran).

Reflections — Perhaps more in seminary on motivation, how to manage volunteers, practicality of administration.

Career: *Assistant Rector and Coordinator of Youth and Adult Education, All Saints' Church, Atlanta, Georgia, 1984-present; Deacon, All Saints', 1983-84.*

Relationship with other clergywomen: *Good when able to get together; all fairly independent.*

Sources invigorating ministry: *The ministry itself; the pursuit of preaching.*

Theological Interests: *Homiletics, theological fiction (reading and writing): Graham Greene, Flannery O'Connor, Frederick Buechner.*

Reaction to preaching: *Wonderful; people want copies.*

Suggestions for those considering ministry: *Be certain ordained ministry is calling and, if so, then preserve, tenaciously.*

Activities/Interests: *Freelance feature writing, fancy cooking, running.*

INDEX